THE GREAT RUBBER STAMP BOOK

THE GREAT RUBBER STAMP BOOK

Designing
Making
Using

DEE GRUENIG

Sterling Publishing Co., Inc. New York

A Sterling/Chapelle Book

— DEDICATION & SPECIAL THANKS—

I want to dedicate this book to my students everywhere whose support and enthusiasm have encouraged me to experiment and create. And, to my husband, Warren, whose presence made it all possible.

I would like to acknowledge and thank my creative assistant, Lynne Taylor, and gifted colleague, Colleen Hamil, for their help and support, and special recognition to Sue Nan Douglass for sharing her secrets for carving eraser stamps and to Janet Yamano for her flair with fabrics!

I would also like to thank the following companies and manufacturers for providing materials that were used in this publication: The Art Institute, Clearsnap, Dalee Bookbinding Company, E & K Success, Enchanted Creations, Family Treasures, Fiskar, Gick Publishing (Make-A-Memory frame and album kits), Hunt Manufacturing, Innovation Specialties, Mark Enterprises, Posh Impressions, Ranger Industries, Rubber Stampede, Sakura Color Products, Stamp Francisco, Tsukineko, and Uchida Marvy.

Chapelle: Jo Packham, Owner • Cathy Sexton, Editor
Hazen Photography: Kevin Dilley, Photographer

If you have any questions or comments or would like information on specialty products featured in this book, please contact Chapelle, Ltd., Inc., P.O. Box 9252, Ogden, UT 84409 • (801) 621-2777 • (801) 621-2788 Fax

If Rubber Cement is not available in your area, consult with any local crafts store to find a comparable product.

Library of Congress Cataloging-in-Publication Data
Gruenig, Dee.
    The great rubber stamp book : designing, making & using / by Dee Gruenig.
        p.   cm.
    "A Sterling / Chapelle book."
    Includes index.
    ISBN 0-8069-1397-5
    1. Rubber stamp printing. I. Title.
TT867.G78 1996
761--dc20   96-4990
                                    CIP

10 9 8 7 6 5 4

Published by Sterling Publishing Company, Inc.
387 Park Avenue South, New York, NY 10016
© 1996 by Chapelle Ltd.
Distributed in Canada by Sterling Publishing
c/o Canadian Manda Group, One Atlantic Avenue, Suite 105
Toronto, Ontario, Canada M6K 3E7
Distributed in Great Britain and Europe by Cassell PLC
Wellington House, 125 Strand, London WC2R 0BB, England
Distributed in Australia by Capricorn Link (Australia) Pty Ltd.
P.O. Box 6651, Baulkham Hills, Business Centre, NSW 2153, Australia
All Rights Reserved
Sterling ISBN 0-8069-1397-5
Printed and Bound in U.S.A.

About the Author

Mention her name to anyone who rubber-stamps, and you will probably find "instant" recognition. Dee's legendary zeal is contagious! Periodicals have called her "the head cheerleader of rubber stamping," and her quest remains to take stamping out of just a simple stamp pad mentality, into the extraordinary world of multi-colored art.

She is noted for her overflowing innovation. This includes the creation of numerous new accessories for stamping, original stamping methods, entertaining instruction, best-selling stamp designs, and industry leadership. Her well-known bold line of rubber stamps, **Posh Impressions**, appears in stores worldwide.

Dee has a master's degree in art education from Stanford University, and she originally put it to use teaching art as a public school teacher. Though she loved teaching, the business world was calling to her.

In 1984, she opened her first of three California retail stores, **Posh Presents**, in Laguna Niguel. In 1992, a second store, **Posh Impressions**, opened in Brea. Then in 1995, a similar, but larger **Posh Impressions** opened in Irvine, complete with a studio for Dee and her staff to continue their innovative efforts.

Over a sixteen year period, Dee has personally taught more than 50 types of stamping classes to approximately 30,000 students in her own or in other retail stores. She has instructed many more through appearances in four videos, two of which she produced herself, by speaking to large enthusiastic crowds at numerous conventions, by appearing on such television shows as ABC's popular **"Home Show,"** and through articles in a number of publications. A particular honor for Dee was the United States Army requesting her to teach rubber stamping to the art directors of 22 PX Exchanges in Europe when they converged in Wiesbaden, Germany (photo album pages are shown below).

She has also found time to serve on the advisory boards of the **National Stationery Show** and *Gifts and Decorative Accessories* magazine, but Dee's favorite activity continues to be researching what more can be done with a rubber stamp!

Dee and her husband, Warren, live near Laguna Beach, California.

CONTENTS

TOOLS OF THE TRADE

Descriptions of More Than 40 Commonly Used Tools

Rubber Stamps

Artistic expression has exhibited itself since cave drawings. The creation of rubber stamps has brought art without anxiety and, because most of us still enjoy coloring, rubber stamping is a perfect art form.

To children, rubber stamps are toys or learning tools. To adults, they are practical, inexpensive, versatile implements for making things more colorful and personal.

Rubber stamps come in many shapes and sizes, and they are usually mounted on wood, foam, or on rollers. Rubber stamps bring color and creativity to a level that anyone can master!

Stamp Pads & Textile Ink

Rainbow pads, of the hand-dyed variety, offer a fabulous blend of colors. Some of the dark colors used in rainbow pads tend to stain rubber stamps and brayers.

Pigment ink pads have an ingredient in them that makes the ink dry much slower. The colors in pigment-based rainbow pads will not blend with each other, so they stay perfectly separated. One of their biggest advantages is that the slow-drying inks allow time to add embossing powders that need to be heat-set. Pigment inks may be used without powders only on porous paper. If used on glossy paper without powder, it will never dry. Pigment pads come in many colors, including metallic, and are also available in white and in clear.

One-color basic stamp pads with a felt surface are best used on outline design stamps which will be colored in with pens once the ink is dry. The ink is water-soluble and quick-drying.

Textile inks are specially formulated for use with fabrics. They are permanent and washable. The ink should be spread onto an un-inked foam pad before it is used. They also are available in a dabber-type bottle that can be applied directly onto the stamp.

Markers

Dual-tip water-base markers have a smaller size brush tip on one end and a fine writing tip on the other. Use the brush tip for coloring inside an outline type stamp design, or finer details on the rubber stamps. Use the fine tip for touch-ups and for writing or line accents.

Water-base felt brush-tip markers are the workhorses of color blending. The size of the brush tip applicator determines the speed of the color application.

Pens

White correction pens are used for white writing and for accenting. Use one specifically with a ball or roller-ball point applicator. The correction fluid dries quickly and has a wonderful opaque quality over dark backgrounds.

Permanent micron-tip pens are best for detailing, such as dots and "beeline" marks. They are also used for butterfly trails.

Scroll brush pens have a brush tip on one side and a double tip on the other. It is a split-edge calligraphy tip, slightly unequal, used for decorative bordering and creative line enhancements.

Water-base double-tip pens have a bullet tip on one end and a finer tip on the other. They give a nice variation of size, especially for "wallpaper-lined" backgrounds and for handwriting details.

Embossing pens come with various tips: fine, medium, wide, and calligraphy. They are filled with clear, slow-drying embossing ink. Embossing powder must be added to the ink and heated.

Calligraphy pens come in brilliant colors and double tips for multi-options. Different size lines are useful for writing as well as bordering enhancement and wide striped lines.

Papers, Sticker Papers, Stamp Positioner & Paper Cutter

Glossy coated paper is usually best for stamping. The inks stay on the surface for brighter colors. Porous and textured papers soak up the ink and therefore the colors do not look as brilliant.

Card stock is heavy-weight paper. Several sizes and shapes are available pre-packaged for stamping purposes. Larger sizes can be found at most crafts stores or through paper suppliers.

The stamp positioner is similar to a T-square and is usually made from a clear lucite material. It is used with a tracing-type see-through paper which can be purchased at stamp stores. The purpose of the stamp positioner is to place a stamp in precisely the position it is desired.

Paper cutters make the cutting of papers and mats precise and easy. They have a grid surface with ruler measurements across the top edge. The long blade, attached to the handle, pulls down against the side edge.

Sticker paper comes in a variety of sizes and finishes. It has a peel-off backing over a sticky back. Sticker paper is used to make sticker paper overlays as detailed on page 25. Sticker paper can be purchased in permanent or removable. It is recommended that the permanent be used on projects that will be handled, such as projects to be mailed. For the brightest colors when stamping, use a sticker paper with a glossy surface.

Foam Board & Films

Foam board is available in several thicknesses and colors. It is made from a very light-weight styrofoam material pressed between a paper top and bottom. A very sharp cutting blade is necessary for cutting foam board or it will "ball up" or tear unevenly.

Fabric transfer film is a heat-sensitive film made to be used in or with color copiers. It has a paper backing which is peeled off after the image has been heat-pressed onto the desired piece of fabric, such as a T-shirt, dress, or sweat suit.

Drafting film is a clear sticky film with a peel-off backing for use with black-and-white copiers. Drafting film makes a clear sticker with black details. Outline designs work best and can be placed over glittery vinyl peel-and-stick film to make glitzy stickers.

Brayers

The soft rubber brayer is the most commonly used brayer for creating backgrounds. Ink the entire surface of the brayer by rolling it over hand-dyed rainbow pads. Brush markers can also be used to color the soft rubber brayer. While the brayer is resting on its handle, apply the markers to the rubber roller as it is turned. Rubber brayers come in 2", 4", and 6" widths.

The black foam brayer is made from a hard-textured sponge-type material, and because of its texture, a softer look is rendered. Ink the entire surface of the brayer by rolling it over hand-dyed rainbow pads. Brush markers can also be used to color the black foam brayer.

The sponge brayer is made of a soft sponge material and has a plastic handle. These brayers are very inexpensive. Use brush markers to color the surface of the brayer in random patterns; then spray it with a light mist of water. Roll it over a stamping surface to create a watercolor background.

Sponges, Compressed Sponges &
Loose-Textured Ribbons & Lace

Good quality wedge-shaped makeup sponges can be used with brush markers to create several effects. Color one edge of the sponge, and blot lightly to test the color intensity. Dabbing the sponge around the edge of artwork gives a soft air-brushed look. Dab over and over without blotting for darker color, or place down on the stamping surface and pull it across for a streaked look.

A compressed sponge starts out as a large sponge, but is com-pressed down to about 2" x 2" x 1". Because of its density, it holds a lot of ink and is great for mak-ing streaked patterns. Compressed sponges are much harder than makeup sponges.

Loose-textured ribbons and lace can be used as stencils when used with markers, sponges, and/or brayers. Because of the texture, very interesting backgrounds can be created.

Glues & Adhesives

Double-stick tape is sticky on both sides and available at most crafts stores. It is best used with heavier papers; two light-weight sheets taped together might have a ridge from the tape.

Spray adhesive comes in a can. Spray the back of the artwork and mount it on another surface. Take care in mounting — once it's mounted, it cannot be changed.

Rubber cement is used in this book as an art tool, rather than as an adhesive. Refer to "Rubber Cement Resist Techniques" on pages 45-48.

Glue pens have various styles of tip applicators. The ultrafine tip, bullet tip, and flat edge work best. Glue pens dispense a tacky drying glue which holds glitter or embossing powder, as well as adheres papers together.

Embossing Powders & Heat Tool

Embossing powders are available in many opaque colors, as well as metallic, irridescent, and sparklers, which contain glitter. These powders are poured over pigment inks. The excess should be shaken off, and the powder is then set using a heat tool.

Heat tools are made for embossing. They get very hot, but they do not blow much air. Therefore, a hair dryer will not work.

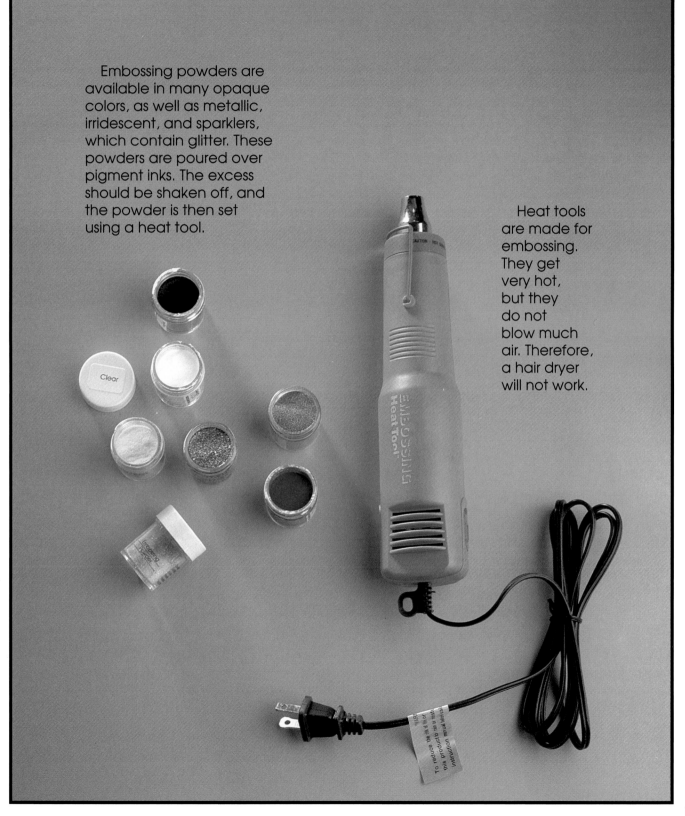

Glitters & Heat-Resistant Double-Stick Tape

Ultrafine designer glitters come in dozens of luscious colors. Glitters can be used over heat-resistant double-stick tape, but they are especially recommended to be used with designer adhesive when glitter writing and for making artistic accents on greeting cards.

Designer adhesive is a specially formulated industrial-strength glue that dries clear and stays dimensional. It is used to hold ultrafine glitters permanently so that they cannot rub off.

Heat-resistant double-stick tape is oftentimes referred to as "wonder tape." It is a distortion-free double-sided, extra sticky tape that comes in several widths. It has a protective covering that peels off easily and can be used for foiling, embossing, and glittering, as well as adhering almost anything together permanently.

Decorative Scissors, Fancy Punches & Other Tools

Decorative scissors are scissors that have unique edges which make fancy cuts instead of straight ones. They are available in a variety of styles and add special finishing touches to any artwork.

A twisting spatter brush is a round brush that looks similar to a bottle brush with a wire handle and a wooden rod that is turned to create the "spattered" ink look over artwork.

Fancy punches make more than just holes! They are available in many different shapes, including hearts, trees, stars, and cows. Some are designed with several shapes to go around corners. Fancy punches are available in metal squeeze-handle styles and in small plastic squares with thumb presses.

A stylus is basically a handle with a blunt metal point on each end. A stylus is used for scoring fold lines. Simply lay a metal-edged ruler across paper where a fold should be and run the stylus along the edge of the ruler.

A precision cutting tool has a plastic or metal handle that holds a very sharp narrow blade. This tool is utilized for cutting when scissors simply are not appropriate.

GETTING STARTED

The Basics of Stamping & Blending

Simple Stamping

The examples shown were done by coloring the rubber stamps with brush markers. Blending colors should be done from lightest to darkest tones. After applying the darkest color, go back over the line where the colors meet with the lighter color to blend them.

Exhale on the stamp's surface to re-moisten any ink that has started to dry; then position it on a stamping surface and press firmly for several seconds. The larger the stamp, the more pressure should be applied.

When the stamped image is complete, clean the stamp thoroughly with a mixture of half water and half window cleaner sprayed on a clean rag or cleaning pad. Dry the rubber stamp before applying more color.

If, for instance, a yellow lemon slice is stamped, and the next color is to be orange, or if a light shade of one color should graduate into darker shades of the same color, there is no need to clean the stamp between stampings.

Stamping Components

Geranium

Mums

Iris

Sunflowers

Fuchsia

Oriental
Basket

Forget-Me-Nots

Rose

Foxglove

Blending Colors

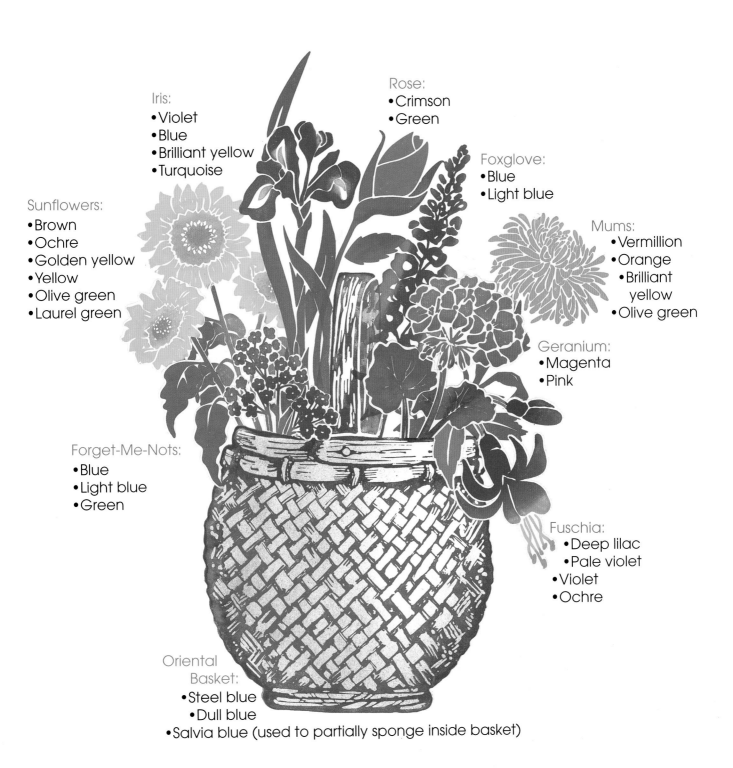

Iris:
- Violet
- Blue
- Brilliant yellow
- Turquoise

Rose:
- Crimson
- Green

Foxglove:
- Blue
- Light blue

Sunflowers:
- Brown
- Ochre
- Golden yellow
- Yellow
- Olive green
- Laurel green

Mums:
- Vermillion
- Orange
- Brilliant yellow
- Olive green

Geranium:
- Magenta
- Pink

Forget-Me-Nots:
- Blue
- Light blue
- Green

Fuschia:
- Deep lilac
- Pale violet
- Violet
- Ochre

Oriental Basket:
- Steel blue
- Dull blue
- Salvia blue (used to partially sponge inside basket)

... From Simple to Stunning! Using brush markers and solid surface stamps.

How to Make the Best Impression

Lined Image vs. Bold Image

The most basic rubber stamp available is an outline design that gives an open area that can be left white or colored in like a coloring book image.

Try taking stamping to a new designer level with bold images that have large surface areas by coloring and blending colors right on the rubber before stamping.

Once the image has been stamped, the artwork is complete!

Whole Image Masking

Thoroughly apply ink to a rubber stamp. Stamp the stamping surface; then stamp the same image onto a piece of paper. Carefully cut the image out of the paper, and use it to "mask" over the image stamped on the stamping surface. Using an inked rubber stamp, continue stamping, pressing hard enough to get a good impression over the raised layer of paper. When finished, remove the mask and enjoy the results.

Streaking

Thoroughly apply ink to a rubber stamp. Stamp the stamping surface. Without lifting the stamp from the stamping surface, pull it in the opposite direction of the way the image should appear to be going. This streaking effect gives the illusion of motion. Do not use this technique on glossy paper!

Fading Out

Thoroughly apply ink to a rubber stamp. Stamp the stamping surface. Without re-inking, continue stamping until all ink has been used — exhaling on the stamp will help accomplish this. The warm, moist air will reactivate the ink that has dried on the stamp. This technique gives depth and adds interesting light and dark shades.

Sticker Paper Overlays

Sticker paper is available with a high-gloss finish, a semi-gloss finish, and a satin finish. It also is available in both permanent and removable varieties.

It can be purchased in 8 1/2" x 11" sheets or prepackaged in smaller sizes. Because it has a peel-off backing, it is perfect for stamping on to make custom stickers.

Begin by stamping any image or greeting on sticker paper. Using scissors, cut the images out, leaving a narrow border. This tiny white border will help coordinate with the white lines in the stamp designs, as well as make the sticker stand out. It also makes it easier to cut the sticker out.

When placing sticker paper overlays on artwork, they can be placed on one at a time or several can be stuck together first. If desired, create an arrangement before sticking them onto the background surface. This gives the option of adding to or changing the design before it is permanently part of the finished artwork.

Stickers made from removable sticker paper can carefully be peeled off and reattached and are wonderful for making

a master to keep filed or for making pieces that will be laminated. However, when using removable sticker paper, be aware that the edges sometimes lift up on their own and therefore are not suitable for projects that will be handled frequently or mailed.

BACK-GROUND & ACCENT TECHNIQUES

General Directions & Stamping Ideas

Brayer Techniques

These techniques can be used on surfaces to create different background patterns. The directions below help illustrate the application of these backgrounds. The process can be done to create backgrounds including stripes, wiggles, confetti, and plaids, as well as landscapes and florals. Reversing images is also a part of this technique and is explained on page 29. When completed, the background will be colorful, festive, soft, or scenic.

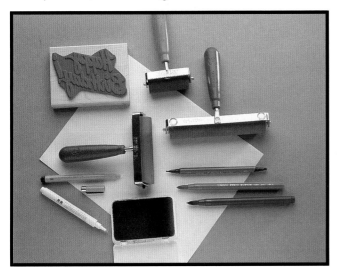

SUPPLIES NEEDED: Soft rubber brayer (2", 4", and 6"), brush markers, fine-point markers, rainbow stamp pad, calligraphy pens, white correction pen, rubber stamps, and a stamping surface.

STRIPES: Using markers, make stripes on a 4" or 6" brayer (resting on its back), while turning the roller so the stripes go all the way around and meet themselves. Roll the brayer across the stamping surface in the desired direction.

WIGGLES: Repeat process for making stripes (above), but instead of making straight lines, make wavy lines on the brayer.

CONFETTI: Using the tips of markers, randomly make small marks in different directions over the entire surface of the brayer. Roll the brayer across the stamping surface in the desired direction.

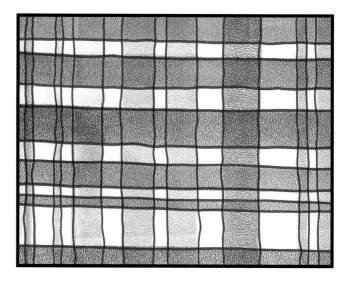

PLAIDS: Using markers, make stripes on a 4" or 6" brayer, while turning the roller so the stripes go all the way around and meet themselves. Roll the brayer across the stamping surface. Re-ink as necessary for desired intensity. Repeat in the opposite direction.

ENHANCED PLAIDS: To enhance the plaid pattern, outline the stripes with a fine-point marker after the pattern has been applied to the stamping surface. Allow plaid pattern to dry before outlining. For best results, follow the edges of the lines — do not use a ruler.

RAINBOW PAD PLAIDS: Using a rainbow stamp pad, thoroughly ink a 2" brayer by rolling it over the pad several times. Roll the brayer across the stamping surface, pressing hard, until all the ink has been used and the surface has been filled. Re-ink as necessary for desired intensity. Repeat in the opposite direction. Shadows and highlights can be added with the tips of brush markers or calligraphy pens and a white correction pen.

RAINBOW PAD BACKGROUNDS: Using a rainbow stamp pad, thoroughly ink a 4" brayer by rolling it over the pad several times. Roll the brayer across the stamping surface, pressing hard, until all the ink has been used and the surface has been filled. Re-ink as necessary for desired intensity. Be sure to turn the stamping surface around to match up the rainbow pattern of color.

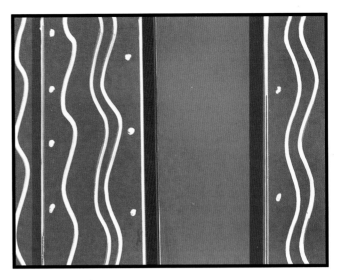

RAINBOW PAD LANDSCAPES: Using markers, color a rubber stamp (such as a tree). Lay the stamp down, colored side up, and roll a clean rubber brayer over the image several times. Roll the brayer over a dry rainbow pad background. Re-ink and repeat as necessary for desired effect. Stamp rain over images and grass or sand in the foreground.

WHITE PEN CONTRAST: Using a white correction pen, make lines or designs over a dry rainbow pad background. If desired, add dark shadows using the tips of brush markers.

REVERSE IMAGE LANDSCAPES: Using markers, color a rubber stamp (such as a tree or a mountain). Lay the stamp down, colored side up, and roll a clean rubber brayer over the image several times. Roll the brayer over the stamping surface several times to get the images as thick as desired. Clean the brayer, and repeat process with a foreground image (such as sand, water, or rocks).

REVERSE IMAGE FLORALS: Using markers, color a rubber stamp (such as a large floral). Lay the stamp down, colored side up, and roll a clean rubber brayer over the image several times. Roll the brayer over the stamping surface several times to get the images as thick as desired. If desired, re-ink the stamp and stamp directly on the stamping surface for a bright enhancement.

Stamping Ideas Using Brayer Technique: Stripes

Stamp tickets, sports equipment, and a greeting on sticker paper. Cut out, leaving a narrow border. Place all sticker paper images on a brayered striped background, overlapping as desired.

Stamp an arrangement of peppers and a greeting on sticker paper. Cut out, leaving a narrow border, and place on a brayered striped background in a "tumbling" pattern.

Stamp a brayered zig-zag pattern on sticker paper. Stamp a vase over the brayered pattern and cut out. Stamp an arrangement of flowers and a greeting on sticker paper. Cut out, leaving a narrow border, and place on a brayered striped background. Arrange greeting so it overlaps onto the vase.

Stamp slices of watermelon and a greeting on sticker paper. Cut out, leaving a narrow border, and place on a background of small stripes close together for a great contrast. Overlapping images adds depth to any stamped artwork.

Stamping Ideas Using Brayer Technique: Wiggles

Stamp hot air balloons and a greeting on sticker paper. Cut out, leaving a narrow border, and place on a brayered background.

Stamp a vase over a sticker paper wavy striped brayered background. Stamp irises on sticker paper. Cut out, leaving a narrow border, and place on a zig-zag brayered background.

Stamp seed packets on sticker paper to make simple, but spectacular, overlays on any brayered background. Stamp seed packets and peppers or flowers on sticker paper. Cut out, leaving a narrow border. Arrange peppers or flowers in the center of the seed packets, overlapping, as desired. Use a calligraphy pen or marker to label the seed packets with the appropriate contents. The pepper seed packet shown above was placed on a brayered background design made up of straight lines and zig-zags, which creates a "Southwest" look. The floral seed packet shown on page 32 was placed on a brayered confetti background.

Stamping Ideas Using Brayer Technique:
Confetti

Stamp ink bottles, a pen, and a greeting on sticker paper. Cut out, leaving a narrow border, and place on a brayered background so they appear to be "dancing" across the background.

Brayered confetti makes the perfect background for anything stamped for a party!

Stamp watermelon slices and sunflowers on sticker paper. Cut out, leaving a narrow border, and place on a brayered background. Use a calligraphy pen or marker to add a greeting or stamp one directly on the background.

Stamping Ideas Using Brayer Technique:
Plaids

Stamp labels or vases and flowers on sticker paper. Cut out, leaving a narrow border, and place on a simple brayered plaid background for a fabulous look. Arrange flowers, overlapping, as desired. Use a calligraphy pen or marker to add a greeting, or stamp one directly on the stamped label or vase.

Stamped images can be placed on backgrounds that have been brayered with the plaid design going in horizontal or diagonal directions.

Stamp "confetti" to get the look used inside the Western label on the left. Use a calligraphy pen or marker to add a greeting, or stamp one directly on the stamped label.

Stamping Ideas Using Brayer Technique:
Enhanced Plaids

Stamp labels or vases and flowers on sticker paper. Cut out, leaving a narrow border, and place on a simple brayered plaid background for a fabulous look. Enhance the look by outlining the plaid lines to get a bolder image. Arrange flowers, overlapping, as desired. Use a calligraphy pen or marker to add a greeting, or stamp one directly on the stamped label or vase.

Stamping Ideas Using Brayer Technique:
Rainbow Pad Plaids

Stamp a basket and apples on sticker paper. Cut out, leaving a narrow border, and place on a rainbow pad plaid background. Baskets of fruits and eggs are very easy to cut out.

Use a fine-point brush marker or white correction pen to lightly define the lines of the plaid background. Stamp pinecones, ribbons, and a greeting on sticker paper.

Stamping Ideas Using Brayer Technique: Rainbow Pad Backgrounds

Use sticker paper overlays, ranging from a simple seed packet (above) to layers of cutout scenery images (below). Place them on a brayered rainbow pad background — the fastest and easiest background to create.

Stamping Ideas Using Brayer Technique: Rainbow Pad Landscapes

Brayered and stamped details make spectacular scenes on these rainbow pad skies. Images can be stamped directly on the background, such as buttes and/or mountains. A touch of fantasy can be added by using white embossing powder and/or a white correction pen. Images can be stamped on sticker paper and cut out, leaving a narrow border. Arrange on brayered backgrounds, overlapping, as desired. The stickers are a bold enhancement to any landscape design.

Stamping Ideas Using Brayer Technique:
White Pen Contrast

Stamp a sports label on sticker paper in a free form design. Cut out, leaving a narrow border, and place on a brayered background with white pen contrast. Stamp a greeting inside the label.

Stamp a vase and flowers on sticker paper. Cut out, leaving a narrow border, and place on a brayered background with white pen contrast in a zig-zag pattern. A white embossed greeting is the perfect accent.

Stamp a vase and flowers on sticker paper. Cut out, leaving a narrow border, and place on a brayered background with white pen contrast in a simple wavy-line pattern. Use brush marker shadows to give this design its classic look.

Stamp a vase and flowers on brayered sticker paper. Cut out, leaving a narrow border, and place on a brayered background with white pen contrast in a zig-zag pattern. Use brush marker shadows to give this design its bold look.

Stamping Ideas Using Brayer Technique: Reverse Image Landscapes

Brayered trees and grass with darker stamped accents couldn't be easier or more beautiful! Lightly sponged grass will make green colors even richer.

Brayered trees and grass make an instant forest — pretty enough to frame! Try using some unusual colors — grass isn't always green. The evening sun creates a rainbow of hues.

Stamp some sunflowers on sticker paper. Cut out, leaving a narrow border, and place on a brayered bamboo background, overlapping as desired.

Stamp some fences, flowers, a birdhouse, and birds on sticker paper. Cut out, leaving a narrow border, and place on a brayered background, overlapping as desired. The sticker paper images create the foreground for this landscape design.

Stamping Ideas Using Brayer Technique:
Reverse Image Florals

Create a bright brayered background of flowers. Stamp a label and two flowers on sticker paper. Cut out, leaving a narrow border. Place label on background, and add the two flowers, positioning as desired. Stamp a greeting in the center of the label, or use a pen or a marker to write in a personal sentiment.

Create a brayered background of fuschias. Add a few dot accents and stamp raindrops to announce any shower! Stamp a few brightly colored fuschias on sticker paper. Cut out, leaving a narrow border, and place on brayered background. The brightness will help make these fuschias stand out from the background. Stamp a greeting in the corner of the artwork.

Stamp a greeting in a bold color over a field of brayered carnations. Keep in mind that the brayer will reverse the direction of the stamped image. This technique is perfect to use when stamping flowers — it is quick and easy and it allows the flowers to lean both ways!

Pen Enrichment Techniques

These techniques can be used on surfaces to create different accents and background patterns. The directions below help illustrate the application of these techniques. Borders and frames for your stamped artwork, or personal sentiments, can be added with pens. Pen accents can also be used to create backgrounds that resemble wallpaper.

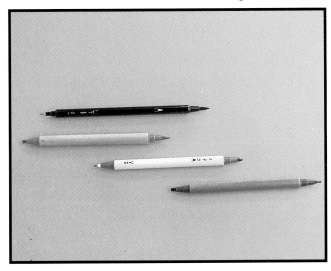

SUPPLIES NEEDED: Beveled-edge ruler (not pictured), scroll pens, calligraphy pens, fine- and medium-point pens, and bullet-point pens.

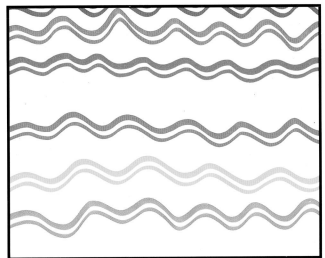

SCROLL PENS: Using a scroll pen, make two lines at once. When making straight lines, a beveled-edge ruler used upside down helps prevent dragging.

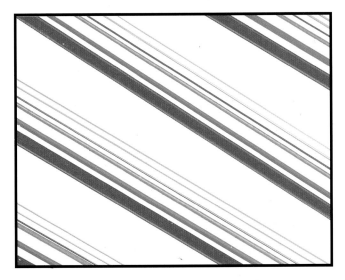

WALLPAPER: Using a fine- or medium-point pen or a calligraphy pen (or a combination), make lines. A beveled-edge ruler used upside down helps prevent dragging. Lines can be straight or diagonal, can cross for a checkered look, and can be spaced evenly or unevenly.

BORDERS & FRAMES: Using a scroll pen, make a border around the artwork. To border a greeting, stamp the greeting and then use a scroll pen to border it, starting and ending on each side of the words as illustrated on page 44.

Stamping Ideas Using Pen Enrichment Technique: Scroll Pens

Use a beveled-edge ruler to achieve the look above. Turn the ruler upside down to prevent the scroll pen from dragging, thus getting the cleanest lines possible. Use a fine- or medium-point pen to write a greeting around the outside edges of any border.

Use a scroll pen to make wavy freehand lines, like the ones shown above. Use the same technique over a lightly brayered striped background, as shown below. Stamp the vase, basket, and flowers on sticker paper.

Stamping Ideas Using Pen Enrichment Technique: Wallpaper

Use a combination of wide- and fine-point pens, evenly spaced, to achieve this look.

Use a wide-point calligraphy pen and a ruler to make the squares shown above.

Pen accents highlight the artwork for a festive look. Place custom stickers as desired.

Use a fine-point pen, evenly spaced, and in two directions, to get the look above.

43

Stamping Ideas Using Pen Enrichment Technique: Borders & Frames

Borders and frames are easily made using scroll pens. Simply make straight or curved corners. When using sticker paper overlays, make the border around the perimeter of the artwork area first. After stamping the overlay images, cut out, leaving a narrow border. Position them, overlapping, as desired. When stamping a greeting, stamp the words first, then make the border lines around them.

Rubber Cement Resist Techniques

These techniques create a background look like no other. Stamping over the rubber cement once it has thoroughly dried allows unique, one-of-a-kind patterns to be created after the rubber cement has been rubbed off.

SUPPLIES NEEDED: Rubber cement, soft rubber brayer (4" or 6"), brush markers, rainbow stamp pads, sticker paper, and a stamping surface.

OVER WHITE PAPER: Brush rubber cement over the stamping surface in straight, wavy, or diagonal lines in one or two directions. Allow to dry thoroughly. Ink a rubber brayer with a rainbow pad or with brush markers in a zig-zag pattern. Roll over stamping surface. Once ink has dried, rub the rubber cement off.

SPOTLIGHT WITH DOUBLE COLOR: Use paper that has been treated with a watercolor or zig-zag brayered background. Brush rubber cement in the center only. Allow to dry thoroughly. Ink a rubber brayer with dark colored brush markers in a zig-zag pattern. Roll over stamping surface. Once ink has dried, rub the rubber cement off.

OVER LIGHTLY BRAYERED STAMPING SURFACE: Repeat process for stamping over white paper, but use paper that has been colored with a light watercolor or rainbow pad background.

45

Stamping Ideas Using Rubber Cement Resist Technique: Over White Paper

Using the brush from the rubber cement, make diagonal brush strokes across the surface.

Using the brush from the rubber cement, make brush strokes in two directions, leaving space in between.

Using the brush from the rubber cement, make wavy brush strokes across the surface of the artwork, leaving space in between. Use the basic watercolor technique over the top of the rubber cement. Stamp Mardi Gras masks and a greeting on sticker paper. Cut out, leaving a narrow border. When rubber cement is dry, rub off and place sticker paper overlays on top, positioning and overlapping as desired.

Stamping Ideas Using Rubber Cement Resist Technique: Spotlight with Double Color

Bright center "spotlights" can be very dramatic!

Stamp the vases of flowers, the palm trees, and the hibiscus blossoms on sticker paper. Cut out, leaving a narrow border. Place on stamped backgrounds, positioning and overlapping, as desired.

Stamping Ideas Using Rubber Cement Resist Technique: Over Lightly Brayered Stamping Surface

Using the brush from the rubber cement, make brush strokes as desired over a lightly brayered background. Add sticker paper overlays as desired. Greetings can be made from sticker paper or stamped directly onto the artwork. Experiment by using more than one technique at a time!

Sponging Techniques

These techniques can be used on surfaces to create different background patterns. The directions below help illustrate the application of these backgrounds. The process can be done to create backgrounds with heavy solid color, stenciling, streaking, sponging, as well as an airbrush effect. When completed, the background will be either solid or patterned and have either a striking or a subtle appearance.

SUPPLIES NEEDED: Makeup sponge, compressed sponge, rubber stamps, sticker paper, brush markers, scratch paper, spray bottle with water, and a stamping surface.

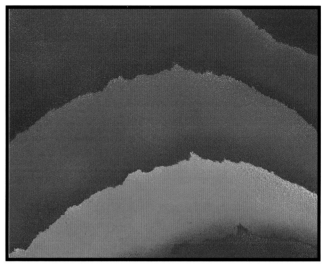

HEAVY SOLID COLORING: Color the end of a makeup sponge with a marker. Dab sponge over stamping surface until color is solid. To achieve this look, sponge over torn paper.

AIRBRUSHING: Color the end of a makeup sponge with a marker. Dab sponge on scratch paper until airbrush texture appears — sponge will be almost dry. Dab sponge over stamping surface several times. Airbrushing softens edges and fills in open areas.

STENCILING: Using a rubber stamp, stamp the same images on stamping surface and on sticker paper. Cut out images from removable sticker paper. Place stickers over exact images on stamping surface. Sponge around stickers to desired shade and remove stickers.

49

STREAKING: Mask an area on stamping surface, and color the end of a makeup sponge with a brush marker. Starting at the edge of masked area, pull sponge across stamping surface and repeat.

RIBBON SPONGING: Color the end of a makeup sponge with a brush marker. Dab sponge over ribbon or loose-weave netting to create textures.

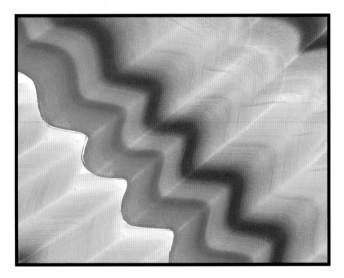

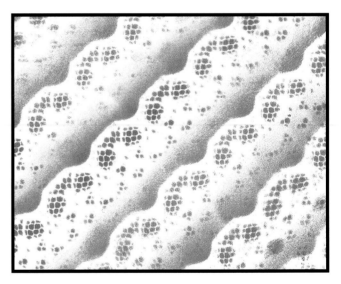

COMPRESSED SPONGING: Color both sides of a corner edge on a compressed sponge with a brush marker. The sponge will soak up a generous amount of ink. Starting at the outside edge of the stamping surface, pull the sponge across it, holding the paper down tightly. Repeat process several times before re-inking sponge. If a wet look is desired, the colored corner edge of the sponge can be lightly sprayed with water before applying to stamping surface. Be sure to use paper underneath to catch the excess color!

LACE STENCILING: Color the end of a makeup sponge with a brush marker. Dab sponge over lace to create textures with an entirely different look.

Stamping Ideas Using Sponging Technique: Heavy Solid Coloring

Stamp the "stardust swishes," followed by sponging. The area between the swishes should remain blank. Stamp hearts on sticker paper. Cut out, leaving a narrow border, and place on background. Stamp the word "Love" on top of each heart.

Use sticker paper masks to protect the stamped clouds while sponging the sky. Complete the design by stamping a label and several buildings on sticker paper. Cut out, leaving a narrow border, and place on background. Stamp a greeting on the label, or use a pen or marker to write one by hand.

Stamping Ideas Using Sponging Technique: Airbrushing

When creating beach scenes, like those shown at the left and below, light sponging helps soften the sky, the sand, and the water. Use sticker paper overlays as desired.

Use a reverse paper mask to protect the outer areas while sponging the inside of the bags, below.

Stamping Ideas Using Sponging Technique: Stenciling

Stamp the clouds. Cover with sticker paper or paper masks to protect them while sponging the sky. If desired, clouds can be lightly sponged once the masks have been removed.

To create a soft color for grass and sand, lightly add sponging.

Stamping Ideas Using Sponging Technique: Streaking

Use sticker paper masks to keep the center rectangles protected while streaking. Stamp

greeting and other images inside the rectangles once the masks have been removed.

Color-copy the above artwork, and use it as a party invitation for any "hot" occasion!

Stamping Ideas Using Sponging Technique: Ribbon Sponging

To create these backgrounds, start by coloring a clean, damp brayer (4" or 6") with brush markers; make zigzag lines close together. Roll the brayer over a loose-weave fabric that has some of the threads removed, such as abaca.

Sponge loose-weave netting on sticker paper. Stamp a vase on top and cut out. Stamp flowers on sticker paper, and cut out, leaving a narrow border. Place vase and flowers on a brayered striped background.

This technique can be used on sticker paper followed by an open image stamp, like the jar at the top. The vase above was created by using the basic watercolor technique shown on page 68.

Sponge loose-weave netting to create a background. Stamp slices of watermelon, flowers, and a greeting on sticker paper. Cut out, leaving a narrow border. Place images on ribbon-sponged background.

Stamping Ideas Using Sponging Technique: Compressed Sponging

Use pastel-colored ink to make a heavenly background for this sticker paper angel and her label greeting.

Stamp flowers and a greeting on sticker paper. Cut out, leaving a narrow border, and place on compressed-sponge background.

Use a very dry sponge to create the look above. Dry sponges produce white streaks and add an interesting texture. Emboss the leaves on a dark paper.

Use a spray bottle with water to lightly moisten an inked sponge to create the look shown at the left. Pull the sponge in straight or wiggly lines.

Stamping Ideas Using Sponging Technique:
Lace Stenciling

Wide lace can be used to create a look similar to the sample shown in the upper left-hand corner. Narrow lace can be used to create a look similar to the other two samples shown. Sponge the color over the lace. Stamp remaining images on sticker paper. Cut out, leaving a narrow border, and place on lace stenciled background, positioning and overlapping as desired.

Textured Background Techniques

These techniques can be used on surfaces to create different background patterns. The step-by-step directions below help illustrate the application of these backgrounds. The process can be done to create backgrounds of dots, splatters, and brush strokes, as well as creative clusters, as shown below. When completed, the background will be full of multi-colored clusters (dots, splatters, or brush strokes) and will have a fabulous visual mixture of colors.

Creative Clusters

SUPPLIES NEEDED: Rubber stamp to be used as background pattern, stamp pads or brush markers, and a stamping surface.

STEP ONE: Mask the center. Using a light colored stamp pad or brush markers, ink stamp and randomly stamp surface two or three times. Repeat as many times as necessary.

STEP TWO: Using a slightly darker colored stamp pad or brush markers, re-ink stamp and randomly stamp surface two or three more times. Repeat as many times as necessary.

STEP THREE: Using a darker accent colored stamp pad or brush markers, re-ink stamp and randomly stamp surface two or three more times. Repeat as many times as necessary.

Once the chosen background pattern has been stamped on the stamping surface, a sticker paper overlay can be applied to the stamped surface. This overlay will cover much of the background pattern, but completes the design by giving a focal point. Stamping ideas using the textured background technique and sticker paper overlays are shown on pages 60-63. For step-by-step directions for making sticker paper overlays, refer to page 25.

Dots

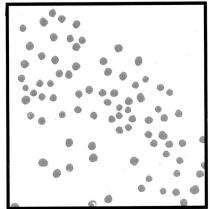

Splatters

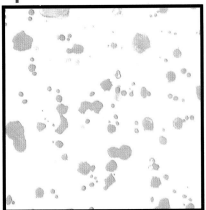

Brush Strokes

Stamping Ideas Using Textured Background Technique: Creative Clusters

Stamp around a masked area in rows of different colors.

Stamp background using square desk notes to give a white frame border when stamped around. Stamp several times before re-inking.

Stamping Ideas Using Textured Background Technique: Dots

Stamp cake, poppers, and greeting on sticker paper. Cut out, leaving a narrow border. Place on a background of colorful dots, and, if desired, soft-sponge to add "bursts" to the multi-colored dots.

To make dot pinwheels, apply pressure to the stamp. Count to three and twist the stamp in the desired direction. This helps create an illusion of motion.

Stamping Ideas Using Textured Background Technique: Splatters

Stamp background with a splatter pattern. Use the splatter stamp conservatively for the look above, or generously for the look below.

Stamp background with a splatter pattern. Stamp vase and roses on sticker paper. Cut out, leaving a narrow border. Arrange as desired and place on the stamped surface.

Stamping Ideas Using Textured Background Technique: Brush Strokes

To achieve a streaked look, use a matte-finish paper stamping surface. A glossy finish will not work. Ink stamp and press down on one edge. Holding down firmly, pull stamp across the surface. For a lighter streak, repeat process before re-inking.

Stamp background in rows using different colors. Stamp two or three times before re-inking. Use a paper mask in the center.

Twisting Spatter Brush Techniques

These techniques can be used on surfaces to create different background patterns. The directions below help illustrate the application of these backgrounds. The processes can be done to create streaked backgrounds enhanced by spattering and sponging. The backgrounds can be enhanced by using one or more background applications. When completed, the background will be contemporary and have a fabulous graphic visual effect.

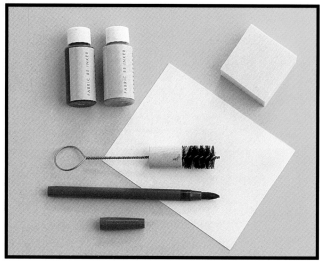

SUPPLIES NEEDED: Twisting spatter brush, compressed sponge, bottled ink, brush markers, and a stamping surface.

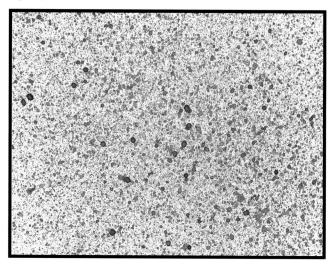

SPATTERING: Dip twisting spatter brush in bottled ink. Shake off excess. Turn wooden rod to make spatter pattern on stamping surface. Can also be applied over streaks.

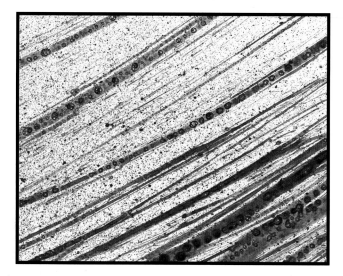

STREAKING: Dip twisting spatter brush in bottled ink. Shake off excess. Gently pull brush across stamping surface.

SPONGING: Allow streaks to dry. Color compressed sponge with a brush marker. In the same direction, gently pull sponge across stamping surface over streaked lines. If desired, change colors using streaks to separate.

Once the chosen background pattern has been stamped on the stamping surface, a sticker paper overlay can be applied to the stamped surface. This overlay will cover much of the background pattern, but completes the design by giving a focal point. Stamping ideas using the twisting spatter brush technique and sticker paper overlays are shown below and on pages 66-67. For step-by-step directions for making sticker paper overlays, refer to page 25.

Stamping Ideas Using Twisting Spatter Brush Technique:
Streaking

Sponging over streaking adds a softness to any piece of artwork.

Stamp background by streaking in two directions to make a dramatic image burst with color.

Stamping Ideas Using Twisting Spatter Brush Technique: Sponging

Sponge in two colors and allow a little white to show in between. Add a sticker paper label, custom made to match, with balloons, confetti, and hand-drawn outlines.

Sometimes it is nice to use only small sticker paper overlays, allowing the beauty of the background to be enjoyed. Sponge with the flow of the streaked lines in a rainbow of colors to get a bright, spectacular look!

Streak and sponge this background in two directions to create a checkered look. Overlapping colors can create the look of an entirely new color! Stamp a sticker paper label with a greeting to provide the center of interest.

Sponge this background with three colors. Stamp the hearts and the greeting on sticker paper and airbrush the hearts. Cut out. Leave a narrow border, if desired. Place hearts and greeting on colorful background, positioning and overlapping as desired.

Stamping Ideas Using Twisting Spatter Brush Technique: Spattering

Mask the center. Use a rubber stamp of splatters for the large spots, and then spatter the entire stamping surface using a twisting spatter brush.

Watercolor Techniques

These techniques can be used on surfaces to create background patterns resembling watercolor. The directions below help illustrate the application of these backgrounds. The processes can be done to create soft, muted backgrounds and/or loud, bright backgrounds. The backgrounds can be enhanced by using one or more background applications.

SUPPLIES NEEDED: Sponge roller, black foam brayer, brush markers, spray bottle with water, creative cluster and splatter rubber stamps (not pictured), rainbow stamp pad, paintbrush, and a stamping surface.

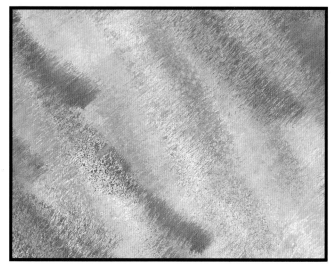

BASIC WATERCOLOR: Using the tips of brush markers, randomly make horizontal marks over the entire surface of the sponge roller. Lightly spray roller with water. Roll the sponge across the stamping surface in the desired direction.

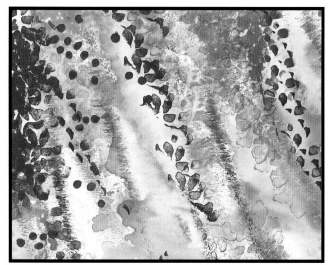

ENHANCED WATERCOLOR: Using a stamp pad or brush markers, color creative cluster or splatter rubber stamp. Stamp images on stamping surface over dry watercolor background. Paper may warp when wet, but will dry nearly flat.

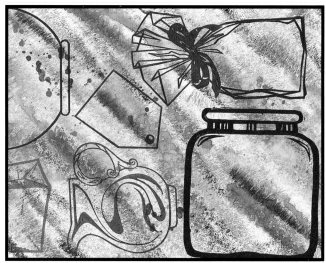

WATERCOLOR OVERLAYS: Repeat process for basic watercolor onto sticker paper. When dry, stamp over the color with a darker color and cut out.

BRUSH-ON WATERCOLOR: Using a wet paint-brush, touched lightly on a brush marker to pick up a small amount of ink, brush ink onto a stamped image(s).

FOAM BRAYER WATERCOLOR: Using markers, color a black foam brayer. Roll over stamping surface to get a soft, speckled look. Because the surface of the brayer is black, it is difficult to see the ink.

Stamping Ideas Using Watercolor Technique: Basic Watercolor

Stamp petunias on sticker paper. Cut out, leaving a narrow border. Arrange in an oval on a basic watercolor background. Stamp a greeting in the center directly onto the watercolor.

Stamp a watercolor background. In complementary colors, stamp roses on sticker paper. Cut out, leaving a narrow border. Place roses on watercolor as desired, and stamp the words onto the invitation.

Stamping Ideas Using Watercolor Technique:
Enhanced Watercolor

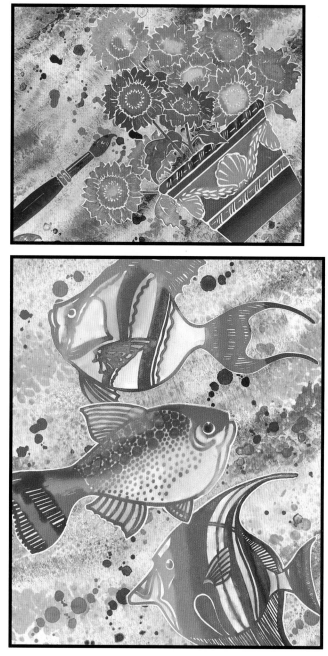

Stamp fish on sticker paper, and lightly color them with a wet paintbrush. Cut out, leaving a narrow border. Place on watercolor background that has been accented with creative clusters and splatters.

Stamp a two-tone watercolor background — sky tones on top and earth tones below. Stamp the mountains directly onto the background, but stamp the fence, cacti, cow skull, and roadrunner on sticker paper. Cut out, leaving a narrow border. Arrange as desired on the desert scene.

Stamping Ideas Using Watercolor Technique:
Watercolor Overlays

To create fabulous watercolor vases, prepare a watercolor background on sticker paper. Allow to dry. Stamp an open lined image on top of the watercolor background. Cut out and place on any background. Stamp flowers on sticker paper and cut out. Arrange flowers in vases.

Stamping Ideas Using Watercolor Technique: Brush-On Watercolor

Use a wet paintbrush with a little ink from a brush marker to fill in an open lined image.

The effect is a softer color than would be achieved if only markers had been used.

Create a dot background. Stamp pansies onto sticker paper. Watercolor them using the brush-on technique. Arrange over the dot background.

Stamping Ideas Using Watercolor Technique: Foam Brayer Watercolor

Brayer a rainbow pad background. Add zig-zag stripes with a soft rubber brayer. Stamp fish bowl and fish onto sticker paper. Cut out, leaving a narrow border. Place fish bowl on background, and stamp a greeting inside. Arrange fish as desired. Use a combination of rubber stamps to get custom greetings!

Brayer a background in a zig-zag pattern with lines in between. Stamp confetti and words onto brayered background. Stamp balloons onto sticker paper. Cut out, leaving a narrow border, and place as desired. Use a pen to add the strings if cutting the strings out is not desired.

Brayer a background that has been lightly sprayed with water. When dry, stamp grass over background. Stamp the basket, eggs, and some extra grass onto sticker paper. Cut out, leaving a narrow border. Arrange images as desired, and stamp a greeting on the background.

Brayer a rainbow pad background. Add wiggly stripes with a soft rubber brayer. Stamp the angels and the word onto sticker paper. Cut out, leaving a narrow border. Arrange images as desired.

Embossing

These techniques can be used on surfaces to create images with the texture and sparkle that add richness to any artwork. Embossing is a technique for the creative — beautiful images can be created using one-color embossing powder or many colors for the brightest, most festive of looks. It is almost like magic — the heat tool magically melts the powder.

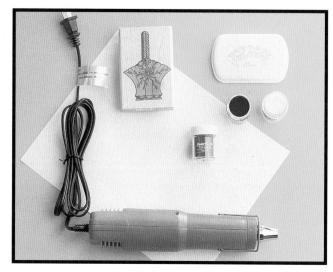

SUPPLIES NEEDED: Rubber stamps, embossing ink pads or slow-drying pigment pads, heat-sensitive embossing powders, a heat tool (light bulbs and toasters will work, but a hair dryer will not), and a stamping surface.

ONE-COLOR EMBOSSING: Stamp an image using an embossing pad. Pour on embossing powder and tap off excess. Heat with heat tool until the powder melts — the color and texture will change.

MULTI-COLOR EMBOSSING: Stamp an image using an embossing pad. Pour on embossing powder, only covering the areas to be the first color. Tap off excess, always away from the unpowdered part of the stamped image.

Repeat with remaining embossing powder colors until the entire image has been covered with embossing powder. Heat with heat tool until the powder melts — the color and texture will change.

"THIS IS YOUR LIFE!"

Glitter Writing

These techniques can be used on surfaces to create written images (and simple shaped images, such as hearts and stars) with the lustre of glitter. Glitter writing is simple — just remember to write in a smooth continuous motion, with the entire arm, not just the wrist!

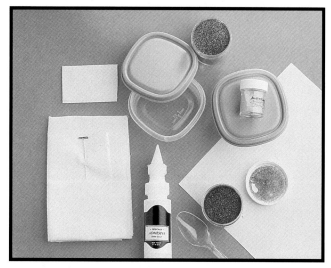

SUPPLIES NEEDED: Designer adhesive, designer glitter, a spoon, glitter trays (with lids), 2" stick pin or safety pin (for cleaning tips), a scrap of cloth, cardboard (for scraping off mistakes), and a writing surface.

APPLYING THE ADHESIVE: Gently shake bottle. Touch tip to the writing surface and gently squeeze bottle, moving it in a smooth continuous motion. Release pressure on bottle, remove tip, and clean it with a scrap of cloth.

ONE-COLOR GLITTER: Using a spoon, sprinkle the glitter over the adhesive. Tap off excess back into glitter trays.

MULTI-COLOR GLITTER: Using a spoon, sprinkle the glitter over the adhesive, only covering the areas to be the first color. Tap off excess, always away from the unglittered glue, back into glitter trays. Repeat with remaining glitter colors until the entire image has been covered with glitter.

Foam Block Stamping

This technique can be used on any painted, stained, or unfinished surface to embellish it. It is best to use a water-based stamping medium that is made specifically for foam block stamping. The stamping medium most often used is a glaze that has a subtle transparency and will create its own shadings.

SUPPLIES NEEDED: Water-based stamping medium, soft foam blocks, flat paintbrush, and a stamping surface.

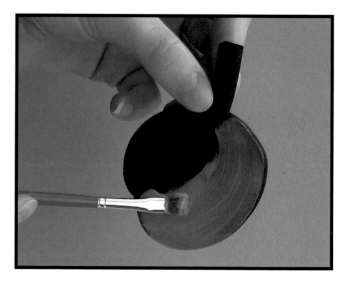

LOADING THE STAMP: Hold the block by the handle. Using a flat paintbrush, apply a coat of stamping medium to cut side of block. Brush medium out to the edges, avoiding the handle area.

STAMPING: Holding the block by the handle, gently stamp onto stamping surface. Once the block is in place, release the handle. Press the block down with fingertips.

REMOVING THE STAMP: Holding the block by the handle, carefully remove it from the stamping surface. Repeat process. After two or three impressions are made, reload the block with stamping medium.

Doors

Stamping on Glass

This technique can be used on glass surfaces to embellish pieces of glass — bottles, jars, mirrors, and windows. It is best to use a permanent nonporous hard surface ink that is made specifically for stamping on glass surfaces. These inks are generally fast drying; therefore, mistakes and/or stray marks need to be cleaned up immediately using an ink solvent.

SUPPLIES NEEDED: Glass cleaner, nonporous hard surface inks, clean un-inked foam stamp pad, rubber stamps, glass stamping surface, scratch paper, ink solvent, and a towel.

PREPARING GLASS SURFACES: Using glass cleaner, clean all glass surfaces that will be stamped. Allow to dry thoroughly.

STAMPING: Practice stamping the images onto paper. When perfected, stamp the images onto the glass as desired, pressing firmly.

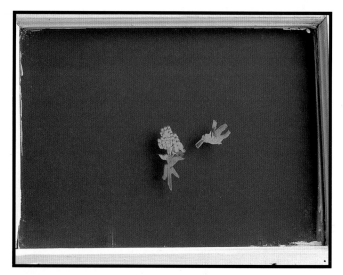

TO AVOID SMEARING: Be careful not to press too hard. If the stamp should turn, even slightly, the image will smear. If the image is repeated more than 10 times, clean the stamp after every tenth impression.

Glass Bottles & Jars

Stamping on Wood

This technique can be used on wooden surfaces to embellish pieces of wood — finished or unfinished. It is best to use a permanent nonporous hard surface ink that is made specifically for stamping on wooden surfaces, but water-based paints can also be used. The hard surface inks are generally fast drying; therefore, mistakes and/or stray marks need to be cleaned up immediately using an ink solvent, but make sure the finish on the wood will not be affected.

SUPPLIES NEEDED: Sandpaper, nonporous hard surface inks or a water-based stamping medium, clean un-inked foam stamp pad, rubber stamps or foam block stamps, wooden stamping surface, scratch paper, ink solvent, and a towel.

PREPARING WOODEN SURFACES: If wooden surfaces are not smooth, use sandpaper to sand until all surface areas are smooth. Clean dust off using a tack cloth or a towel. If desired, stain or paint wood and allow to dry thoroughly.

STAMPING: Practice stamping the images onto paper. When perfected, stamp the images onto the wood as desired, pressing firmly.

TO AVOID SMEARING: Be careful not to press too hard. If the stamp should turn, even slightly, the image will smear. If the image is repeated more than 10 times, clean the stamp after every tenth impression.

Wooden Caddy

Stamping on Walls

This technique can be used on any painted or wooden wall surface to embellish it. It is best to use a permanent nonporous hard surface ink that is made specifically for stamping on walls and wooden surfaces, but water-based paints can also be used. The hard surface inks are generally fast drying; therefore, mistakes and/or stray marks need to be cleaned up immediately using an ink solvent.

SUPPLIES NEEDED: Nonporous hard surface inks or a water-based stamping medium, clean un-inked foam stamp pad, rubber stamps, foam block stamps, or sponge stamps, a painted wall, scratch paper, ink solvent, and a towel.

PREPARING WALLS: Before beginning, make sure walls are clean and smooth. If desired, a new coat of stain or paint can be applied, but allow to dry thoroughly.

STAMPING: Practice stamping the images onto paper. When perfected, stamp the images onto the walls as desired, pressing firmly.

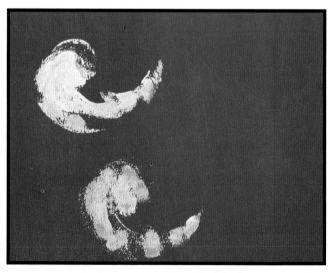

TO AVOID SMEARING: Be careful not to press too hard. If the stamp should turn, even slightly, the image will smear. If the image is repeated more than 10 times, clean the stamp after every tenth impression.

Walls

Stamping on Fabric Directly

This technique can be used on fabric surfaces to embellish them. It is best to use paint, dye, or ink that is made specifically for stamping on fabric. Fabrics must be completely dry to prevent smudging, and incomplete stamped images can easily be touched up using a cotton swab. It is recommended that patterns be created on paper first. Once the design is perfected, stamping can be done directly on the chosen fabric.

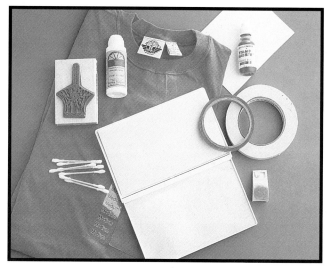

SUPPLIES NEEDED: A smooth-textured fabric item, rubber stamps, fabric paint, dye, or ink, ink solvent, clean un-inked foam stamp pad or makeup sponges, cardboard, cotton swabs, and masking tape.

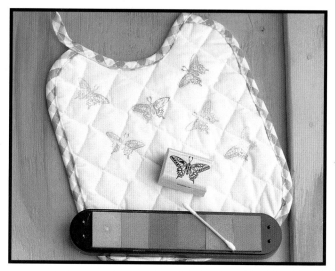

STAMPING PADDED FABRICS: Stamp images directly on padded fabric. Shake clear embossing powder over stamped images and heat with a heat tool to set the ink. Extraneous paint can be removed from stamp edges using a cotton swab before stamping.

STAMPING THIN FABRICS: Place a piece of cardboard under or between fabric layers, and stamp images directly on fabric. The cardboard will prevent any bleed through.

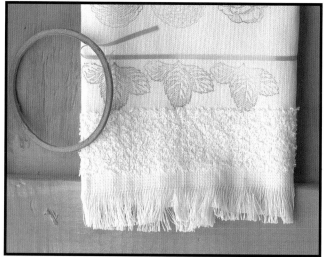

STAMPING LINEAR DESIGNS: Place masking tape on fabric as a guideline for stamping, and stamp images directly on fabric.

Gardener's Delight Apron

Child's Sundress

Child's Sweat Suit & Dress

Stamping on Fabric by Transferring

This technique can be used on fabric surfaces to embellish them. The designs are transferred to the fabric by using a fabric transfer film. Fabric transferring can be done on any number of fabric surfaces, such as clothing and quilt squares. If desired, a peel-and-stick product can be applied to the back of the fabric artwork and adhered to any number of things.

SUPPLIES NEEDED: Stamped artwork, color copier, fabric transfer film, heat press, and a fabric surface. (A T-shirt shop is the best source for finding all the supplies needed to perform this technique.)

CREATING ARTWORK: Create artwork using one, or a combination, of the stamping techniques described in this book.

COLOR COPY TRANSFERS: Once artwork has been created, make a color copy onto fabric transfer film using a color copier. The artwork can be reduced or enlarged as desired, and should be reversed.

HEAT PRESSING ARTWORK ONTO FABRIC: Place fabric transfer film, artwork side down, on fabric surface. Using a heat press, press artwork onto fabric until it has transferred. This should be done professionally — an iron will not work!

T-Shirts

HOW TO CREATE STAMPING DESIGNS

Cutting & Caring for Homemade Stamps

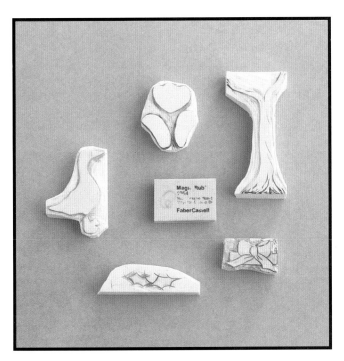

Using an Eraser

Draw or trace a simple design onto tracing paper using a pencil. Place the traced design face down on an eraser, and burnish with a fingernail to transfer the image. Using a sharp knife, cut the eraser to the size that the design will be.

Tint the eraser by stamping it onto a brown stamp pad — the pencil lines will not be affected. Stamp the eraser on paper until it is dry. The tinting of the eraser will allow the cut marks to be more visible.

Using a precision cutting tool, carve away the portions of the eraser that are not part of the design. Then, carefully carve around the design in smooth, decisive lines. Always carve away from fingers and the design.

Next, carve the inner detail. If tiny dots are desired, use a sharp pencil to "jab" holes into the eraser.

If the eraser seems too "tough" to cut, the blade on the cutting tool might need to be changed. As the eraser stamp is being created, frequently stamp impressions onto a scrap piece of paper to refine the image. Do not attempt perfection — imperfection adds character to any stamp!

Using Foam

Foam blocks for foam block stamping are cut from a soft, durable stamping material. The foam used should be easy to clean and can be used repeatedly if proper care is taken.

Using a white tracing pencil, draw or trace the chosen pattern onto the foam. Using industrial scissors or a precision cutting tool, cut the shape from the foam. When cutting a shape, remember to cut a handle. The handle is necessary for stamping and for the removal of the foam block to be done without smearing the stamped image.

If a large project is underway, it is a good idea to stop periodically and wash and dry the foam block before continuing. Once stamping has been completed, wash the foam block with water and dry it between towels.

Refer to "Foam Block Stamping" on page 78 for detailed instructions on how to use foam block stamps and to page 79 for samples of foam block stamping on an ordinary household door.

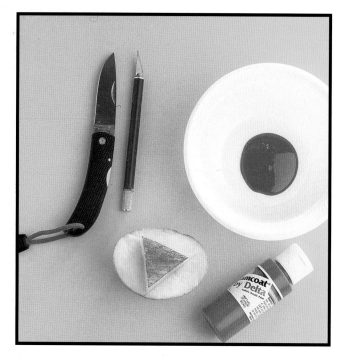

Using a Potato

The potato stamp might be considered the easiest stamp to make — all it takes is a potato and a cutting tool.

Larger potatoes are generally preferred, unless the design being created is especially small.

Begin by cutting a potato in half and set it aside. Draw or trace a simple design onto tracing paper using a pencil, and cut out the design. Place the cutout design onto one of the potato halves, and, holding it securely in place, trace around it using a felt-tip marker.

Using a precision cutting tool, carve around the design. Then, carefully remove the potato around the design. Always carve away from fingers and the design.

Next, carve the inner detail and remove unwanted potato portions.

Simple designs, such as hearts, stars, and diamonds, work best when using potatoes as stamps!

Wash the potato stamp after each color application so that additional colors can be used. Potato stamps can be stored in the refrigerator for up to five days if they are stored in a paper bag.

Using a Sponge

Sponges of any kind can be used to make sponge stamps — makeup sponges, cleaning sponges, and bath sponges to name a few. Using dish-washing sponges works especially well because the "scratchy" backing for scouring can be used as a handle. Compressed-sponge board is also a popular material used for making sponge stamps.

Keep in mind that the texture of the sponge will determine the depth of the stamped imprint. The more dense the sponge, the more solid the image will appear.

When making sponge stamps, simply cut out the design using scissors. Sponge stamps can also be created like potato stamps. Refer to the directions at the left under "Using a Potato."

Simple designs, such as hearts, stars, and flowers, work best when using sponge to make stamps, but more intricate designs can be created or purchased.

Wash the sponge stamp after each color application so that additional colors can be used. When stamping is complete, thoroughly wash out the sponge and allow it to air-dry before putting it away.

CARD CREATIONS & ELEGANT ENVELOPES

Bringing Cards
to Life &
Embellishing
Envelopes

Single-Fold Cards

Single-fold cards are the simplest cards to make. They can open from side to side or from bottom to top and be made any size desired.

Tri-Fold & Multi-Fold Cards

Tri-fold cards have two folds in them. They fold into three sections — the outside sections fold accordion style. They can be made any size desired.

Multi-fold cards have many folds in them; however, there must be an uneven number of folds in order for the card to fold up correctly. They can be made any size desired.

Tri-Fold

Multi-Fold

Pop-Up Cards

Each pop-up requires two folded 4$\frac{1}{2}$" x 6" cards, plus an extra scrap of glossy card stock. Thoroughly apply ink to a rubber stamp. Stamp the "pop-up" image onto the scrap of glossy card stock and cut it out.

On one open card, make two cuts, extending 1" above and below the fold line, about 1" to 1$\frac{1}{2}$"

apart. Score across ends of cuts. Fold, pulling the cut section up to pop it out. If the pop-up image should be off-center or placed at an angle, do not center the cuts described above.

Thoroughly apply ink to a rubber stamp, and stamp the inside of the cut card and the outside of the plain card. Use glue or double-stick tape to adhere the two cards together and to attach the pop-up image.

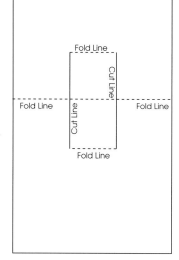

Fold Line

Cut Line

Fold Line   Fold Line

Cut Line

Fold Line

Buds to Blossoms Cards

Cut double-sided glossy card stock to 5" x 12¹/₂". Score on the outside edges of center line only, leaving card unscored in the center where the "buds" will be. Use the "Inside Pot" diagram below to trace the pattern of the curve. Trace pots on sticker or other paper and decorate or shade them. Cut out, leaving a narrow border. Stamp a design in the four corners on the front of the card, and stamp a greeting in the center. Place the edges of the pot for inside on the scored line, and lightly trace the curve onto the card with a pencil. Remove and glue the pot for front below the curved line. Leave space for the buds. Cut along the pencil line with a precision cutting tool, and fold so the curve pops up as part of the front. Glue the pot for inside on the inside right along the curved cut line. Stamp flowers on the top part of the card above the pot. Stamp some flowers on sticker paper. Cut out, leaving a narrow border, and arrange, overlapping, as desired. Stamp a greeting on the inside, below the pot.

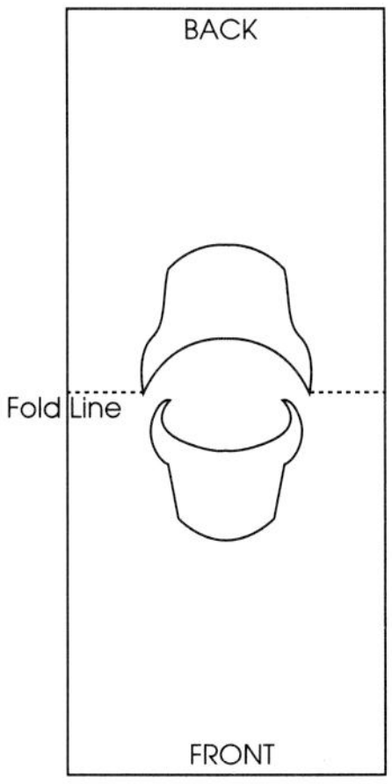

BACK

Fold Line

FRONT

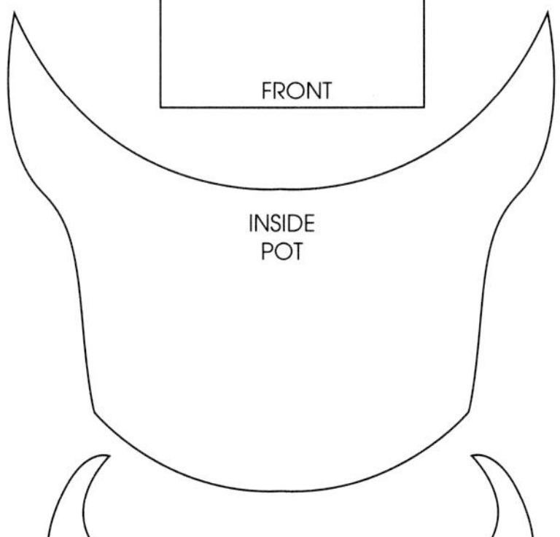

INSIDE POT

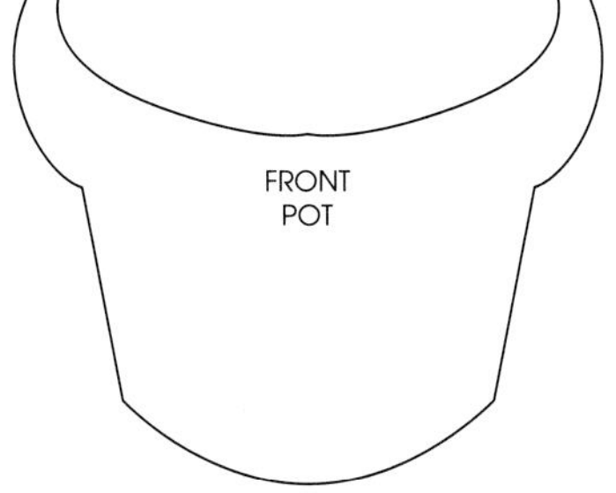

FRONT POT

Explosion Cards

Use double-sided glossy card stock folded to 4¹/₂" x 6". Stamp or brayer the outside of the card and, if desired, the inside too. Add pen lines, handwriting, white correction pen accents, and sticker paper accents as desired. For the inside of the card "explosion" part that goes on the stamp artwork on an 8¹/₂" x 8¹/₂" square of glossy paper (not card stock), but do not embellish with sticker paper overlays. Fold square

according to the directions below. When folded, place double-stick tape or glue on one side of the folded square and adhere it to the center of the inside of the card. Double-check to make sure the design is going the right way before it is glued to the card. Place double-stick tape or glue on the other side of the folded square, and adhere it to the inside of the card.

Begin with a square. Stamp design on square and place right-side up.

Make valley-fold diagonals.

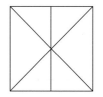

Turn paper stamp-side down, and mountain-fold vertical center. Horizontal-fold if card opens at the bottom.

Let the paper "collapse" into a triangle-shaped base.

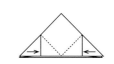

Fold the ends of the top layer of paper to the center. Turn the triangle over, and repeat on the other side.

Unfold last four folds, and reverse-fold, pushing the corners inward.

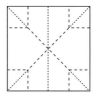

Attach the folded paper to the inside of the card with double-stick tape.

Pinwheel Cards

Cut out pattern on heavy glossy paper stock. Score from the innermost edge of each petal across two petals, as shown in the diagram below, to create a center hexagon (on the front of the card). Stamp a greeting in the hexagon, and stamp a design around all the edges. If desired, stamp the back of the card. Score the center of each petal from the pointed tip to the hexagon by lining up the points directly opposite each other using a ruler. Pinch each of the petals on the scored line from the back side and push it inward. This will make the hexagon lines fold in the opposite directions. Bend each folded petal to the right, and flatten to form a pinwheel.

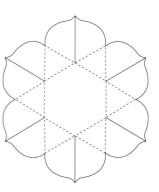

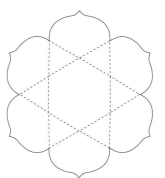

Enlarged Foam Board Postcards

Stamp artwork on glossy white paper or card stock. Using a color copier, enlarge artwork to desired size. Make a second color copy of the same artwork, but in reverse, if the artwork will go on the back of the postcard.

Laminate both copies. Place double-stick tape on the back side of one of the copies, and place it on ¼" foam board. Using a precision cutting tool, die-cut around the artwork, leaving a ⅛" to ¼" border of white around the edges. If using artwork on the back of the postcard, place double-stick tape on the back side of the reversed artwork. Cut out the artwork for the back of the postcard, leaving a ¼" to ½" border of white around the edges. Carefully place the foam board on the back of the design. Because the border should be slightly larger than the border around the artwork on the front, it needs to be trimmed with the precision cutting tool.

Using a permanent marker, write a personal message on one side and address the postcard on the other. If desired, the writing can be done prior to laminating.

Because of the bulkiness of the postcard, additional postage will be required. Purchase self-stick postage stamps in the correct postage amount, and ask the postal clerk to "hand-cancel" it.

Since the original artwork was color-copied, it can be reused for making additional enlarged foam board postcards or for other stamping projects!

Shaker Window Postcards

Decide on a shape for the "window." It is easiest to choose a symmetrical shape. Stamp the window toward the left side of the postcard. If desired, stamp a border for the address and the postage stamps. Stamp the remaining artwork.

Using a precision cutting tool, cut out the window. Turn the artwork upside down over another card the same size (for the back of the postcard), and trace the window placement. Stamp the back of the postcard, leaving a space to write a personal message.

If making a master, color copies of the artwork should be made at this time.

Trace the window onto foam board, and cut it out using a precision cutting tool. Using double-stick tape, attach a piece of acetate, slightly larger than the window, behind the window openings on both pieces of artwork. If desired, laminate both copies using a heavy laminate. This will eliminate having to place acetate over the windows.

Place double-stick tape on the back side of one of the copies, and place it on $1/4$" foam board, lining up the window cutout. Be sure to tape around the window.

Turn over and fill the window with glitter, candy, or confetti.

Carefully line up the windows, and mount the back side of the postcard using double-stick tape, again taping around the window. If necessary, trim the sides.

Using a permanent marker, write a personal message on one side and address the postcard on the other. If desired, the writing can be done prior to laminating.

Because of the bulkiness of the postcard, additional postage will be required. Purchase self-stick postage stamps in the correct postage amount and ask the postal clerk to "hand-cancel" it.

How To Make Envelopes & Fancy Stickers

To make an envelope to fit virtually any size card, first measure the closed card. Several materials can be used to make envelopes, including paper, card stock, construction paper, and fabric. Determine the material that will be used in making the envelope. Add $1/2$" to both card measurements previously taken.

For example, if the closed card measures 5" x 7", the envelope should measure $5^1/_2$" x $7^1/_2$" when it is folded and closed.

Diaper-Fold Envelope

Use Diagram A as a pattern. The card to fit this envelope must be $7^1/_2$" x $7^1/_2$". Adjust the pattern as necessary. Trace the pattern onto the material to be used for the envelope. Cut out the envelope.

Fold three flaps toward the center of the envelope and glue in place. Make a fancy sticker to seal the envelope.

Large Paper Envelope

Use Diagram B as a pattern. The card to fit this envelope must be 5" x 5". Adjust the pattern as necessary. Trace the pattern onto the material to be used for the envelope. Cut out the envelope.

Fold in the sides of the envelope and glue in place. Fold up the bottom and glue. Fold down the top flap. Make a fancy sticker to seal the envelope.

Fancy Stickers

Either make or purchase an envelope with a contrasting paper to go inside. Cut the paper to fit, reserving all scraps.

Choose a glitzy vinyl color to complement the envelope color. Using a black-and-white stamped image as a master, copy onto drafting film (which has a peel-off backing). Cut it out, leaving some of the excess film all around the image.

Peel off the backing and stick to the chosen piece of glitzy vinyl. Cut around the edges to make a glitzy sticker. If desired, the sticker can be used to seal an envelope.

To make two-tone flowers, copy flower onto drafting film. Cut it out. Cut the center petals out carefully, leaving the remaining petals and excess film in one continuous piece. Peel off the backing, a little at a time, and stick to the chosen piece of glitzy vinyl. Place the center petals on another color of glitzy vinyl and cut them out. Place them in the center of the first glitzy vinyl flower sticker. Cut out entire flower.

If desired, fancy stickers can be placed on a scrap of contrasting paper that has been cut with decorative scissors.

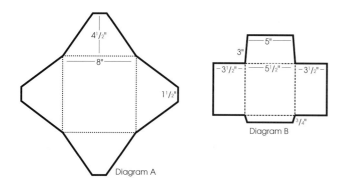

Diagram A

Diagram B

Envelopes & Fancy Stickers

CALENDAR CREATIONS

A Year Full of Colorful Artwork

January

Using a rubber brayer and a ripped paper mask, brayer trees. Then stamp some brighter ones and some snowflakes.

February

Draw hearts on a rubber brayer and brayer a background. Stamp pouch and roses on sticker paper and cut out, leaving a narrow border. Arrange over background.

March

Create a scene starting with a hilltop. Add wild grass, flowers, sunshine, and butterflies. Enhance by sponging and add beelines with a fine-tip pen.

April

Stamp flowers and butterflies. Add beelines with a fine-tip pen.

May

Brayer zinnias and stamp bolder ones over the top. Then stamp hummingbirds.

June

Brayer trees and stamp bolder ones over the top. Stamp ferns at base of trees, and add raindrops over all.

July

Brayer a spangled splatter. Stamp bolder ones over the top. Stamp stars. Stamp flag on sticker paper and cut out. Arrange over background.

August

Brayer cacti and stamp some over the top. Stamp sun. Stamp critters and rocks on sticker paper. Cut out and arrange over background.

September

Brayer some apples. Stamp more apples over the top. Stamp an apple or two on sticker paper. Cut out and arrange over background.

October

Stamp the vines and the sun. Stamp pumpkins on sticker paper. Cut out and arrange. Add stamped spiders, and sponge around the sun.

November

Stamp a bountiful basket.

December

Stamp pine around the edges; then stamp an angel on sticker paper. Cut out and arrange, and add some stars.

GALLERY OF STAMPED PROJECTS

Decorative & Functional Accessories for the Home & Office

Business Card Box, Desk Set & Pencil Case

Embossed City Business Card Box: Emboss a city scape onto off-white card stock. Cut out, leaving a narrow border. Apply wonder tape to the back of the cutout city, and stick onto a purchased business card box.

Fabric Fish Desk Set: Use a sponge roller on sticker paper to replicate basic watercolor. Stamp fish on top of watercolor. Cut out, leaving a narrow border, and place on a white background, positioning and overlapping as desired. Add a few dots or bubbles. Copy artwork onto fabric transfer film using a color copier. Heat-press onto canvas fabric the same color as the purchased canvas desk accessory. Use a peel-and-stick product applied to the back of the canvas artwork, and trim to the exact size. Remove the backing, and press the canvas artwork in place around the desk accessory.

Pansy Pencil Case: Stamp pansies onto sticker paper. Cut out, leaving a narrow border. Cut kraft paper card stock using decorative scissors, and apply spray adhesive to the back. Glue to the top of the purchased pencil case. Stick pansy stickers to the top of the kraft paper, positioning and overlapping as desired.

Checkbooks, Expanding File & Portfolio

Embossed Portfolio: Emboss leaves across the front of the portfolio. Add wonder tape stripes. Remove the protective covering from each stripe, one at a time, and add one color of glitter at a time.

Fish Checkbook Cover: Stamp fish onto glossy paper, and copy onto fabric transfer film using a color copier. Heat-press onto a natural-colored canvas. Use a peel-and-stick product applied to the back of the canvas artwork. Cut out. Remove the backing, and press the canvas artwork in place on the purchased fabric checkbook cover.

Pansy Expanding File: On glossy paper, use the brayer technique with a pansy stamp to create the background. Stamp pansies and fish bowl on sticker paper. Cut out, leav-ing a narrow border. Place fish bowl on top of brayered background. Arrange pansies, overlapping, as desired. Enlarge and reverse onto fabric transfer film using a color copier. Heat-press onto a natural-colored canvas. Cut out. Spray the back of the canvas with spray adhesive, and mount to purchased expanding file. Add ribbon to conceal the edges using wonder tape.

Rose Checkbook Cover: Using textile ink, stamp roses onto a purchased canvas checkbook cover that has been opened up flat. Using a twisting spatter brush and calligraphy ink from a bottle, spatter over the roses and over the entire checkbook cover. Sponge the edges of the cover with textile ink.

Chair Backs & Tabletop

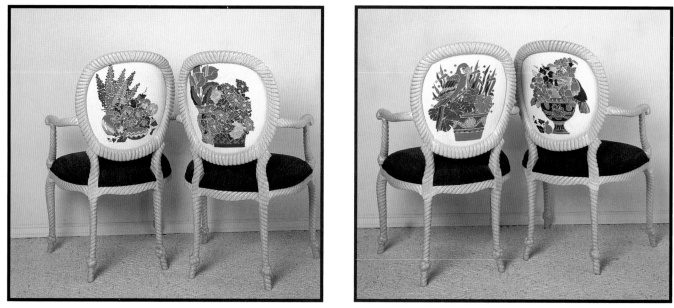

Chairs: Stamp artwork. Color-copy the artwork onto fabric transfer film. Have it heat-pressed onto desired fabric. Fabrics can generally be ordered from furniture manufacturers if a match to other fabrics is necessary.

Cigar Boxes

Western Cigar Box: Cut glossy card stock to fit on top of the purchased cigar box. Brayer the background using a rainbow stamp pad. Add decorative lines with a white correction pen. Stamp a Western frame, six or seven Western borders, four bandanas, and about eight small peppers on permanent opaque sticker paper. Cut out, leaving a narrow border. Stamp a greeting inside the frame. Stick the Western frame on center top of brayered card stock. Place the bandanas in the corners. Add peppers as desired. Using spray adhesive, secure the card stock to the top of the cigar box.

Embossed Roses Cigar Box: Emboss roses and leaves on black card stock. Apply wonder tape to the back, and cut out, leaving a narrow border. Emboss the leaves using two different colors — one color on each side (left and right). Use decorative scissors to trim dusty green and black card stock to fit on the cover, and trim a piece of corrugated cardboard to fit the inside of the colored borders. Using spray adhesive, secure the card stocks together and finally to the top of the cigar box.

Clocks

Artists' Clock: Start with a square of glossy card stock (sample is 9"). Score lightly to find exact center for placement of clock mechanism. Stamp ink bottles in a variety of colors onto sticker paper. Cut out, leaving a narrow border, and place on card stock. Begin with the ink bottles being used at the 12:00, 3:00, 6:00, and 9:00 positions. Arrange the remaining ink bottles to form a circle. If desired, turn ink bottles in different directions. Add ink spots coming out of each bottle. Stamp pen and brush onto sticker paper. Cut out, leaving a narrow border — do not place on card stock yet. Because stamped artwork will fade over time when exposed to prolonged light, it is recommended that a color copy of the artwork be made (pen and brush should be copied to the side of the clock face) — this also allows more than one clock to be created from one piece of artwork. Laminate color copy and mount on cardboard or foam board to stiffen. Cut a hole (approximately 1/4") in the center of the artwork. Attach clock mechanism according to manufacturer's directions. Glue pen and brush onto card stock and cut out. Glue onto actual clock hands, cutting holes where required. Frame clock as desired.

Fruit Clock: Start with a square of glossy card stock (sample is 8 1/2"). Measure diagonally to find exact center for placement of clock mechanism. Using a rubber brayer, create a plaid background. Stamp fruit onto sticker paper. Cut out, leaving a narrow border, and place on card stock to form a circle, positioning and overlapping as desired. Because stamped artwork will fade over time when exposed to prolonged light, it is recommended that a color copy of the artwork be made — this also allows more than one clock to be created from one piece of artwork. Laminate color copy and mount on cardboard or foam board to stiffen. Cut a hole (approximately 1/4") in the center of the artwork. Attach clock mechanism according to manufacturer's directions. Frame clock as desired.

Drawers

Ivy Drawer: Paint the drawer with antique white acrylic paint. Using a precision cutting tool, cut the trellis and the ivy leaves from sponge to make sponge stamps. Stamp trellis on drawer using acrylic paint, working from top left corner. Shade trellis sections with a darker shade of acrylic paint. Randomly stamp the ivy leaves over the trellis. Add vines. If desired, paint the square wooden drawer knob to match the design on the drawer.

Purse Drawer: Paint the drawer with antique white acrylic paint. Tape a small piece of paper at each corner of drawer top, at an angle, to miter corners. Using a purchased purse rubber stamp, stamp purses across the top of the drawer, using a variety of acrylic paint colors. Repeat process for the bottom and sides of the drawer. If desired, acrylic paint can be thinned with an extender.

Flowers & Butterflies Drawer: Sponge the drawer with blue and green acrylic paint. Stamp flowers, butterflies, and leaves onto the drawer with black stamp pad ink. Using prisma-colored pencils, color the flowers, fading from yellow to pink to reds. Color the butterflies with white, blue, and green. Color the leaves with light greens and yellows. Spray with matte clear acrylic spray sealer and add a glass drawer knob.

Framed Artwork & Matching Pillow

IMPORTANT NOTE: Because stamped artwork will fade over time when exposed to prolonged light, it is recommended that a color copy of the artwork be made.

Framed Artwork & Matching Pillow: Create any piece of colorful artwork. This artwork will be used as a master for future projects! Color-copy the artwork onto a good quality gloss paper. Use a paper cutter to cut it out, mak-ing sure it is centered for framing purposes. Frame the artwork as desired using a single or double mat. Use the same master to color-copy the artwork onto fabric transfer film. Have it heat-pressed onto a piece of fabric, and make it into a pillow. Employing the artwork master that has been created, the possibilities for using it are endless!

Guest Register & Sketchbook

"Our Guests" Guest Register: Make three rainbow pad brayered sticker paper stripes. Trim 1/4" stripe off each wide stripe, and set aside. Stamp houses onto sticker paper. Cut out, leaving a narrow border, and place on top of the wide sticker paper stripes, positioning and overlapping as desired. Stick wide and narrow stripes onto white card stock. Write personal sentiments between stripes using a fine-point pen. Copy artwork onto fabric transfer film using a color copier. Heat-press onto a natural-colored canvas. Use a peel-and-stick product to apply to the back of the canvas artwork, and trim to fit. Remove the backing, and press the canvas artwork in place on the purchased book.

Fish Sketchbook: Brayer a background using a rainbow stamp pad. Add pen accents using a white correction pen. Stamp fish on sticker paper. Cut out, leaving a narrow border, and place on a brayered background. Using scissors, cut a turquoise and a plum mat to fit on the cover. Using spray adhesive, secure the card stocks together and the artwork to the top of the card stock. Write words around the outside edge of artwork using a fine-point marker. Copy artwork onto fabric transfer film using a color copier. Heat-press onto a natural-colored canvas. Use a peel-and-stick product applied to the back of the canvas artwork and trim to fit. Remove the backing, and press the canvas artwork in place on a purchased sketchbook.

Gift Bags & Tissue Papers

Calla Lily Gift Bag: Use a rubber brayer on a glossy white gift bag to create a confetti background. To get a firm stamping surface, temporarily remove the gift bag handles, open the bag, and place a box or some books inside. Stamp desired images onto sticker paper. Cut out, leaving a narrow border, and place on gift bag, positioning and overlapping as desired.

Ivy Tissue Paper: Stamp ivy leaves directly onto tissue paper. Images of any shape, size, and color can be used to create decorative tissue paper to accent any gift bag. Stamp tissue paper over extra paper — it will bleed through.

Seed Packet Gift Bags: Stamp seed packets onto sticker paper, and cut out, leaving a narrow border. Write on labels using calligraphy pens. Stamp flowers or fruit onto seed packets and some extras onto sticker paper to be used for overlapping. Cut out, leaving a narrow border, and place on seed packets, overlapping as desired. Remove backing from sticker paper, and place seed packets onto kraft paper. Using decorative scissors, cut around the seed packets, leaving as much border as desired. Using double-stick or wonder tape, stick kraft paper artwork onto gift bags. If desired, tie raffia bows and hot-glue them to the gift bag handles and to the tops of the kraft paper artwork.

Watercolor Gift Bag: Use a sponge roller on a white gift bag to replicate basic watercolor. When dry, enhance watercolor with splatters or creative clusters. Using a rubber brayer and rainbow stamp pad, stamp desired images onto sticker paper. Cut out, leaving a narrow border, and place on gift bag, positioning and overlapping as desired. Frame the design using a white correction pen.

Watermelon Gift Bag: Stamp watermelon slices directly onto a glossy white gift bag or onto sticker paper. If using sticker paper, cut out, leaving a narrow border, and place on gift bag, positioning and overlapping as desired. Using sticker paper allows mistakes to easily be corrected by simply applying the images over the mistakes.

Gift Boxes

Friendly Forest Gift Box: Lay the gift box open flat on a table. Mask the top and bottom sections of the box to keep them white. Ink a tree rubber stamp using markers. Lay it down on table, rubber side up. Run a rubber brayer over the inked tree stamp several times, being careful to position them close to the same level on the rubber brayer. Make sure the trees spread across the width of the brayer. Roll the brayer over the gift box. Repeat for desired effect. Stamp grass in a variety of shades of green across the bottom. Sponge in some sky using a makeup sponge and a cloud stencil. When dry, fold the gift box into position. Apply purchased animal stickers, positioning as desired. Tie gift box with a raffia bow.

Watercolor Kraft Gift Box: Use a sponge roller on a kraft gift box to replicate basic watercolor. Apply watercolor onto all sides and top. Apply watercolor onto sticker paper. When dry, stamp gift bag onto watercolored sticker paper. Stamp flowers onto sticker paper. Cut out, leaving a narrow border. Stick gift bag and flowers onto front of gift box, positioning and overlapping as desired.

Jar Labels

Stamp images onto sticker paper. Make a border or frame using calligraphy pens. Cut out, leaving a narrow border or use decorative scissors. Write on labels using calligraphy or other pens. Remove backing from sticker paper and stick artwork onto jars, positioning as desired. If desired, tie raffia bows and hot-glue them to the labeled jars. Fill the jars as desired.

Ideas:

1) A raspberry label on a jar filled with raspberry-filled hard candies; 2) A sunflower label on a jar filled with sunflower seeds; 3) A watermelon slice label on a jar filled with colored jelly beans, layered to look like a slice of watermelon; 4) A floral label on a jar filled with potpourri; 5) A golfing label on a jar filled with golf tees (not pictured); 6) An artist's label on a jar filled with pens and brushes.

Ideas:

Make labels for home-canned items — use the artwork below by color copying them to the size appropriate for the jar size being used. Write the contents on the labels using calligraphy pens.

Here are some ideas:
- Applesauce
- Apple Butter
- Apple Pie Filling
- Carrots
- Grape Juice
- Grape Jelly
- Jalapeños
- Pie Cherries
- Salsa
- Spaghetti Sauce
- Stewed Tomatoes
- Strawberry Jelly
- Strawberry Syrup
- Whole Tomatoes

Lamp Shade

Seascape Lamp Shade: Trace the pattern for the lamp shade onto glossy card stock. If necessary, two sections will work, but a $^3/_4$" overlap is required. Use a sponge roller to replicate basic watercolor over the entire stamping surface. Along the bottom edge, stamp sea grass and clumps of cacti. Stamp more sea grass and more clumps of cacti in a darker shade. Stamp fish onto sticker paper. If desired, color in or sponge. Cut out, leaving a narrow border, and place on artwork, positioning and overlapping as desired. Add a few dots or bubbles. Copy artwork onto fabric transfer film using a color copier. Cut out transfers and overlap to make one continuous design. Heat-press onto fabric. Cut out, leaving a minimum of 1" border to wrap around edges of lamp shade. Use a peel-and-stick product, applied to the back of the fabric artwork to adhere it to the lamp shade.

Napkins & Placemats

Christmas Tree Napkins & Placemats: Using textile ink, stamp Christmas trees onto matching checkered napkins and placemats in a random pattern.

Ivy Trim Napkins & Placemats: Using textile ink, stamp ivy leaves and vines onto matching natural napkins and placemats to create a border around the outside perimeters. If a stamped border does not come out perfectly, the last image to be stamped can be altered by using a piece of paper masking over the area that has already been stamped and dried to create a partial stamped image.

Photo Frames

Apple Photo Frame: The cardboard on this photo frame has been covered with stamped glossy paper. Stamp backgrounds and images onto the paper as desired. The paper needed to cover the frame should be at least 3/4" larger on all sides to allow paper to be folded over and glued to the back side of the cardboard. Apply rubber cement or spray adhesive to the back of the stamped artwork and to the front of the cardboard. Place stamped artwork onto cardboard. Fold the corners at a 45° angle to make them as neat as possible. Apply rubber cement to the folded corners, and fold over the remaining edges. The backing (stamped with artwork if desired) should be cut approximately 1/2" smaller than frame on all sides to cover. Glue paper to cardboard backing, and carefully center on back of cardboard frame. Glue in place, making sure one side is left open to accommodate the insertion of a photo. If desired, the frame stand can be covered to coordinate with the stamped artwork and glued on so the frame stands horizontally or vertically.

Butterfly Photo Frame: Clean the glass on the photo frame with glass cleaner before stamping. Stamp butterflies onto the glass in the photo frame. Be careful not to press too hard or the stamp will turn and the image will smear. If the image is repeated more than 10 times, clean the stamp after every tenth impression. Refer to the directions for "Stamping on Glass" on page 80.

Falling Leaves Photo Frame: Refer to the "Apple Photo Frame" directions at left.

Umbrella Photo Frame: Stamp umbrellas onto off-white card stock. Stamp clear embossing ink on top of the stamped images using a stamp positioner. Apply clear embossing powder and shake off excess. Heat with a heat tool. Cut out, leaving a narrow border, and temporarily arrange on the photo frame to see where wonder tape should be placed on the back. Areas that will stick up over the photo frame should be left without tape. Apply wonder tape and place on photo frame.

Quilted Wall Hanging & Matching Pillows

Stamp artwork. Copy artwork onto fabric transfer film using a color copier. Heat-press onto desired fabric squares. Turn the artwork into a quilted wall hanging with matching pillows.

Vacation & School Memory Albums

Our Fall Trip Album: Stamp ivy leaves and vines onto sticker paper. Write personal sentiments on top of ivy background using a calligraphy pen. Cut out using decorative scissors, place on corrugated cardboard, and set aside. If desired, the inside front and inside back covers can also be stamped. Cover album, line inside front and back covers, and assemble the album. Use raffia to assemble the album instead of grosgrain ribbon. Refer to the "Our Wedding Album" directions on the opposite page. Glue corrugated cardboard artwork onto the front of the album.

School Memory Album: Use a rubber brayer to stamp apples onto the paper that will cover the front and back of album. Stamp chalkboards onto sticker paper, and cut out, leaving a narrow border. Write personal sentiments on chalkboards using a white correction pen. If desired, the inside front and inside back covers can also be stamped. Cover album, line inside front and back covers, and assemble the album. Refer to the "Our Wedding Album" directions on the opposite page.

Wedding Album

Our Wedding Album: Use a rubber brayer to stamp roses onto the paper that will cover the front and back of album. Spatter the background. Cut a heart from sticker or other paper, using decorative scissors. A fancy punch can be used to enhance the edge of the heart. If desired, the inside front and inside back covers can also be stamped. The paper needed to cover the album should be at least 1" larger on all sides to allow paper to be folded over and glued to the back side of the cardboard. Allow extra length to the paper to accommodate the opening and closing between the cover and the spine. Reinforce the inside areas on both front and back cover papers with masking tape where the cover and spine meet. Apply rubber cement to the back of the stamped cover and to the front of the cardboard. Place the cardboard cover and spine onto the back of the stamped cover paper over the masking tape, leaving $1/4$" space in between. Fold the corners at a 45º angle to make them as neat as possible. Apply rubber cement to the folded corners, and fold over the remaining edges. The inside lining (stamped if desired) should be cut approximately $1/2$" smaller than album on all sides. Carefully center lining on inside front cover, and glue in place. Repeat to line the inside back cover.

Assemble the album by first cutting holes in the front and back covers. Purchased album kits come with the holes in position on the cardboard. Cut an "x" through the paper at each hole, and insert the stamped album pages between the covers, making sure the holes line up. If holes have not been pre-cut, it is important to cut them in the front and back covers so they line up exactly. Using $1^1/2$ yards of $3/8$" grosgrain ribbon and a long, dull tapestry needle, thread the ribbon up through the top hole, around the outer edge, and up through the next hole. Repeat. Bring the ribbon up through the last hole, around the lower edge of the album, and back up through the last hole. Bring the ribbon around the outer edge of the album and back up through the next hole. Repeat. When ribbon is back up to the first hole, bring the other end around the top edge of the album and through the first stitch. Tie a knot and a bow, and trim the excess ribbon.

Wallpaper Borders

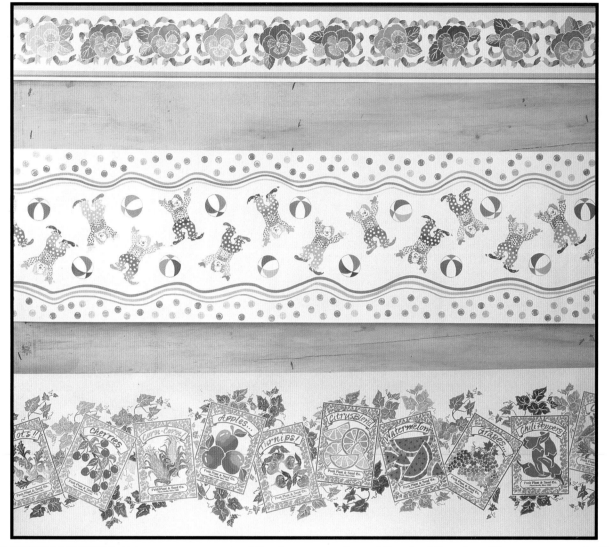

IMPORTANT NOTE: It is recommended that the wallpaper be hung before the stickers are placed. This eliminates the possibility of the stickers getting wet and smearing. It is also important to know that original stamped artwork can be used, but will fade from natural and indirect lighting sources.

Clown Border: Stamp several different, colorful clowns and balls to be used as masters. Color-copy them onto sticker paper. Cut out, leaving a narrow border. Place on purchased pre-pasted plain wallpaper border as desired. Embellish with colorful dots and pen enrichments.

Seed Packet Border: Stamp several different seed packets to be used as masters. Color-copy them onto sticker paper. Cut out, leaving a narrow border. Stamp an ivy background onto purchased pre-pasted plain wallpaper border. Place stickers on wallpaper, overlapping as desired.

Pansy Border: Stamp pansies and leaves in several colors to be used as masters. Color-copy them onto sticker paper. Cut out, leaving a narrow border. Use the pansy and leaf stickers to embellish a purchased pre-pasted ribbon wallpaper border.

Metric Conversions

INCHES TO MILLIMETRES AND CENTIMETRES

MM-Millimetres   CM-Centimetres

INCHES	MM	CM	INCHES	CM	INCHES	CM
$1/8$	3	0.9	9	22.9	30	76.2
$1/4$	6	0.6	10	25.4	31	78.7
$3/8$	10	1.0	11	27.9	32	81.3
$1/2$	13	1.3	12	30.5	33	83.8
$5/8$	16	1.6	13	33.0	34	86.4
$3/4$	19	1.9	14	35.6	35	88.9
$7/8$	22	2.2	15	38.1	36	91.4
1	25	2.5	16	40.6	37	94.0
$1 1/4$	32	3.2	17	43.2	38	96.5
$1 1/2$	38	3.8	18	45.7	39	99.1
$1 3/4$	44	4.4	19	48.3	40	101.6
2	51	5.1	20	50.8	41	104.1
$2 1/2$	64	6.4	21	53.3	42	106.7
3	76	7.6	22	55.9	43	109.2
$3 1/2$	89	8.9	23	58.4	44	111.8
4	102	10.2	24	61.0	45	114.3
$4 1/2$	114	11.4	25	63.5	46	116.8
5	127	12.7	26	66.0	47	119.4
6	152	15.2	27	68.6	48	121.9
7	178	17.8	28	71.1	49	124.5
8	203	20.3	29	73.7	50	127.0

YARDS TO METRES

YARDS	METRES	YARDS	METRES	YARDS	METRES	YARDS	METRES	YARDS	METRES
$1/8$	0.11	$2 1/8$	1.94	$4 1/8$	3.77	$6 1/8$	5.60	$8 1/8$	7.43
$1/4$	0.23	$2 1/4$	2.06	$4 1/4$	3.89	$6 1/4$	5.72	$8 1/4$	7.54
$3/8$	0.34	$2 3/8$	2.17	$4 3/8$	4.00	$6 3/8$	5.83	$8 3/8$	7.66
$1/2$	0.46	$2 1/2$	2.29	$4 1/2$	4.11	$6 1/2$	5.94	$8 1/2$	7.77
$5/8$	0.57	$2 5/8$	2.40	$4 5/8$	4.23	$6 5/8$	6.06	$8 5/8$	7.89
$3/4$	0.69	$2 3/4$	2.51	$4 3/4$	4.34	$6 3/4$	6.17	$8 3/4$	8.00
$7/8$	0.80	$2 7/8$	2.63	$4 7/8$	4.46	$6 7/8$	6.29	$8 7/8$	8.12
1	0.91	3	2.74	5	4.57	7	6.40	9	8.23
$1 1/8$	1.03	$3 1/8$	2.86	$5 1/8$	4.69	$7 1/8$	6.52	$9 1/8$	8.34
$1 1/4$	1.14	$3 1/4$	2.97	$5 1/4$	4.80	$7 1/4$	6.63	$9 1/4$	8.46
$1 3/8$	1.26	$3 3/8$	3.09	$5 3/8$	4.91	$7 3/8$	6.74	$9 3/8$	8.57
$1 1/2$	1.37	$3 1/2$	3.20	$5 1/2$	5.03	$7 1/2$	6.86	$9 1/2$	8.69
$1 5/8$	1.49	$3 5/8$	3.31	$5 5/8$	5.14	$7 5/8$	6.97	$9 5/8$	8.80
$1 3/4$	1.60	$3 3/4$	3.43	$5 3/4$	5.26	$7 3/4$	7.09	$9 3/4$	8.92
$1 7/8$	1.71	$3 7/8$	3.54	$5 7/8$	5.37	$7 7/8$	7.20	$9 7/8$	9.03
2	1.83	4	3.66	6	5.49	8	7.32	10	9.14

Index